TIBBS,

CARRY ON LAUGHING

A Celebration

For Peter Rogers and the late Gerald Thomas

The author would like to thank the following for their help and
support in putting this book together - Dave Sheppard, Clive Banks,
Neil Comer, Marcus Hearn, Caroline Batten, Gary Tillat, Scott Grey,
Simon Buchanan, Rod, Krystyna, Mum, Nichola and Midge.

First published in 1996 by
Virgin Books
an imprint of Virgin Publishing Ltd
332 Ladbroke Grove
London W10 5AH

Thanks to Geoff Tibballs for interviewing Barbara Windsor for the
foreword.

A catalogue record for this book is available from the British Library.

ISBN 1 85227 554 5

Designed by Design 23, London
Printed by Butler and Tanner Ltd, Frome

CARRY ON LAUGHING

A Celebration

Adrian Rigelsford

Virgin

Contents

Foreword

It was a stroke of luck that led to me appearing in the *Carry On* films - a case of happening to be in the right place at the right time. I'd just done a movie with Ronnie Fraser called *Crooks In Cloisters* and he invited me out to lunch at Pinewood Studios. I had arranged to meet him in the bar and to get there I had to walk through the restaurant where Peter Rogers and Gerald Thomas were sitting. It transpired that they were looking for a bubbly blonde for *Carry On Spying* and they decided that I fitted the bill. The series had been going for six years by then and I was really nervous going into something so established, although I was thrilled to be working with people like Kenneth Williams, Charles Hawtrey and Joan Sims, all of whose work I had long admired. The *Carry On* films were very disciplined. It looks like we're all larking about and ad-libbing but there was none of that; you did exactly what was in the script. You might corpse once - which was understandable with Kenny Williams always trying to get you into trouble - but if you did it again they were down on you like a ton of bricks. There was a tremendous camaraderie on set but, surprisingly, not much socialising outside, although I was always very friendly with Kenny. He always used to say he liked me because I was the only one of the team who cleaned their teeth after lunch! Time and money were always tight. The only true location filming I did was two days in Brighton for *Carry On Girls*. The famous bikini scene in *Carry On Camping* was shot in a field at the back of Pinewood in the middle of

winter. It was freezing cold and ankle deep in mud. My top was to be removed by an elderly prop man using a fishing rod and line but on the first take it refused to budge. I shouted to him to stop tugging but he must have been deaf because he just kept reeling me in. The next thing I knew I was being dragged through the mud on my bum!

My favourite *Carry On* was *Henry*, partly because it was the first time I really got to work opposite Sid. People don't realise that Sid was a great song and dance man. I remember seeing him in *Guys and Dolls* when I was 15. For *Carry On Henry*, we had to do a gavotte and, both being dancers, we got it in one take. After that, Sid told Gerald Thomas: 'From now on, I want to play opposite Barbara.' They felt that he would be a bit too old for me - he was 30 years older - but the audience loved it.

The year before he died, Sid told me that out of all the *Carry On* actresses, I'd be the one that everyone would remember. I had to laugh at that because I only did nine of the films, but he may have been right. The day after *Carry On Cleo* was shown on TV recently, a chap came up to me and told me how funny I was in it. I said: 'I wasn't in *Carry On Cleo*.' He said: 'Yes you were.' I don't know how he could confuse me with my friend Amanda Barrie who is tall and dark while I'm small and blonde but he was really insistent and getting quite angry until in the end I had to say: 'Yes, you're right, I was in *Cleo* . . . '

People often ask me why I think the *Carry On* films have remained so popular. I put it

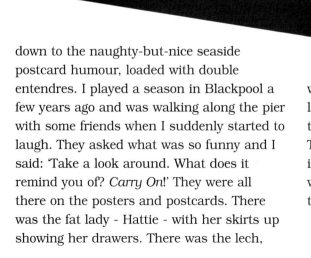

down to the naughty-but-nice seaside postcard humour, loaded with double entendres. I played a season in Blackpool a few years ago and was walking along the pier with some friends when I suddenly started to laugh. They asked what was so funny and I said: 'Take a look around. What does it remind you of? *Carry On*!' They were all there on the posters and postcards. There was the fat lady - Hattie - with her skirts up showing her drawers. There was the lech, which was Sid. There was the little camp man, which was like Charlie and there was the bosomy blonde which was me. That's *Carry On*. A British institution and one which I'm proud to be part of.

Barbara Windsor

Chapter 1

Rudolph Valentino and the Silent Fart

'You may not realise it, but I was once a weak man.'
'Well, once a week is enough for any man.'
Kenneth Williams and Hattie Jacques, *Carry On Doctor* (1968).

There's a joke which still circulates in the film industry about two famous directors sitting in a studio canteen, enjoying the cigars they're smoking as they sit chatting after lunch.

'I saw the latest *Carry On* film last night and you know, there was something quite odd about the whole experience.'

'What? You didn't laugh at one of the jokes, did you?'

'Don't be ludicrous, man! It's just that Kenneth Williams was noticeable by his abscence.'

'Oh, really? He must have been sick the morning they shot that one!'

The *Carry On* films were generally looked upon with scorn and ridicule by a large number of film directors and producers who tended to look down their noses at the series. It was, however, purely a case of jealousy breeding contempt: whilst the art-house brigade of directors slaved for countless months striving to bring their

Hawtrey and Williams in *Carry On At Your Convenience*

visions of cinematic splendour - which few would see or care about - to the big screen, the cheap and cheerful *Carry On* team was happily grinding out productions at the rate of two or three a year. The box-office receipts showed who was more popular, the art-house types or the comedy team, and it was the latter who was raking in bucketloads of cash.

The *Carry On* format obeyed no rules, following only the scriptwriters' imagination. Nobody was safe from ridicule - the army, the police force, the National Health Service and even large-budget epic movies were all sent up something rotten. The barbs were sharp and once they had dug into the latest victim, there was no escape. How many unconfirmed reports are there of patients waking up in hospital, lying face-down with a daffodil inserted into the place where the sun don't shine? The inspiration for that particular prank comes, of course, from *Carry On Nurse*.

A television crew spent a week on the streets of London, cornering members of the public with a camera and asking them to do their favourite impersonation of a celebrity. The vast majority of recorded results consisted of strangled voices screeching out, 'Oooh! No, Matron, no!' Kenneth Williams had made an indelible mark on the consciousness of the British public.

The impact of the *Carry On* style of seaside sauce has had a far-reaching effect and ensured that the films have gone beyond being cult viewing and become part of the British culture. Yet nobody could have predicted in the early days how successful these films were going to be or to how many the series would ultimately stretch. It was all

just a happy and profitable accident.

As each successive film was made, it became clear that a nucleus of comic masters was establishing itself. As the years went by, these comic actors became household names and a large part of their celebrity was due to their work on the *Carry On* films. The popularity of one fed the popularity of the other - both actors and films profited from this symbiotic arrangement.

The on-set antics of this particular troupe of theatrical rogues have also passed into film-making legend. Although this book is liberally spiced with anecdotes from throughout the history of the *Carry On* series, this seems a perfect excuse to list a few extra little gems.

Take, for example, an incident that occurred during the making of *Carry On Cleo*. In the studio lot at Pinewood the cast and crew were taking advantage of the fact that many of the sets for the multi-million

**Carry On Cleo used the sets
from the epic Cleopatra**

dollar epic, *Cleopatra*, starring
Elizabeth Taylor and Richard
Burton, had been left standing
after production had been
completed. The *Carry On* crew
took the opportunity to shoot what
sequences they could for their film
before the lot had to be cleared.

11

Terry Scott suffered for his art in *Carry On Camping*

Charles Hawtrey decided that his elderly mother should see the magnificent sets and took her down to the studio for the day. During a tea break, Kenneth Williams and Joan Sims joined them at their table. As usual, Hawtrey was smoking copiously and only Sims noticed the long strand of ash on his cigarette fall into the open maw of his mother's leather handbag.

'Charles!' she cried, 'your mother's handbag's on fire!'

Without batting an eyelid, he threw the cup of tea he was holding into the bag and closed it, losing not one beat in his conversation.

Another story demonstrates the rivalry that existed between Kenneth Williams and

Sid James. On the set of *Carry On Cowboy*, James was being interviewed by a young reporter. He was explaining why he found it hard to believe that he was actually being paid to dress up in a silly costume and stand around in front of a camera all day. As he pondered on how to expand on the complexities of his job and find a description for it, Kenneth Williams sauntered past, catching the tail end of the conversation. Never one to miss an opportunity to drop an acidic quip, Williams was only too keen to offer his help in finding the right words.

'It's called acting, Sid. You ought to try it some time - you might even find you enjoy it!'

During the filming of *Carry On Camping*, Terry Scott discovered that he had broken out in a painful rash of boils on his behind, but decided that any treatment would have to wait until after he had completed his work on the film.

In the days that followed, he had to spend hours at a time on the back seat of a tandem bicycle, pedalling across bumpy terrain. Later, he had to endure a sequence where a powder flash was detonated in the rear of his cycling shorts when a shotgun was supposedly fired at his bottom. Unfortunately for him, this scene took many takes before it all looked right. Late in the

Sid James goes out looking for Kenneth Williams

night, within the cramped confines of a tent, he also had to endure the indignity and pain of a camera crew shooting a scene where his on-screen wife was removing shotgun pellets from his boil-strewn region. The screams heard in the final film hadn't required any rehearsal!

13

Carry On Laughing

More bottom trouble was encountered on *Carry On Constable*, when the nerves of several lead actors were somewhat on edge due to the fact that a vital scene was about to be shot where their bare behinds were on display. Their characters were to be filmed running out of the showers and along the corridor of a police station clutching nothing but little hand towels to cover their modesty.

After the first take, once a quiet prayer had been offered up at the end of the ordeal, the make-up lady was suddenly summoned to do something about their cheeks for the second take. No, not on their faces. It turned out that the skin tone of the buttocks on view was so pale that it was causing the lights to flare off them. This would have resulted in the actors appearing to have radioactive posteriors on screen.

Kenneth Williams and Leslie Philips in particular had to go through endless reshoots before an appropriate colour match with the rest of their bodies could be achieved. To quote Williams before a radio interview on the subject, 'We had more powder on our behinds than all of the new arrivals in a maternity wing put together!'

Whilst filming on location for *Carry On Cabby*, Sid James vanished during a lunch break - neither he nor his cab were anywhere to be found. When filming began again in the afternoon James reappeared, 'carrying on' as if nothing had happened. Shooting wrapped up for the day and several of the actors cornered him to find out where he had got to. He quickly explained that his disappearance was nothing to worry about. He said that an old lady had got into his cab and asked him to drive her to the local railway station. Not having the heart to tell

her that he wasn't a real cabby, James had driven her there and refused to accept the fare she offered.

Impressed by this good deed, the other actors treated James with a new-found respect. Unfortunately for him, the whole tale was ruined when Charles Hawtrey arrived on the scene, berating James for not stopping to give him a lift on the way back from the local race track. Hawtrey could not

'Oooh! I think I've dropped one!'

to the studio gates, when a sleek black Rolls Royce pulled up alongside him. The passenger in the rear seat wound down the window and called out to him, asking if he wanted a lift. It was Sir Laurence Olivier, who was also halfway through filming at Pinewood. From then on, Olivier gave Hawtrey a lift to and from the bus stop every day until both men finished their work at the studios.

In *Carry On Up the Khyber*, a seduction scene was staged between Kenneth Williams and Joan Sims, involving her gradually succumbing to the considerable charms of Williams as the Khazi of Kalabar. In the middle of a lengthy speech, Williams suddenly let rip with a resoundingly loud and surprisingly ripe fart. The

understand why everybody bar James found his tirade so amusing.

Hawtrey was a strange character who actually liked to travel to and from filming at Pinewood by public transport. This meant that at the start and end of a day's work he would make the long trek to and from the nearest bus stop to Pinewood. On one of the mornings during the making of *Carry On Spying*, he was heading along the pavement

object of his on-screen affections was far from impressed and made her feelings quite clear on the matter, saying that she thought both he and it were disgusting and that she'd never come across anyting like it in her entire career.

'Come off it,' protested an indignant Williams. 'Even Rudolph Valentino had to fart!'

'Yes, Kenneth.' replied the very calm and

dignified director, Gerold Thomas, 'but those were silent films!'

Throughout his career Williams was notorious for his lavatorial humour and for such a private man he could be an alarming exhibitionist. His most frequent habit at the studio was to tuck his private parts between his legs so that it looked like he had changed sex. He called this his 'vagina trick'. He would then wander up to actors, actresses, technicians, cameramen and secretaries and expose his remodelled genitals to see what effect his trick would have on them. They would either laugh in a hysterically embarrassed manner or just stalk off in disgust. One reaction, however, left the normally unstoppable Williams speechless.

During the shooting of *Carry On Henry*, Williams wore an elaborate tunic with flowing robes. This allowed him to simply lift up his tunic to pull his favourite stunt. One afternoon as the tea trolley approached, the front of his robe was hoisted aloft and Williams' pelvic area thrust in the direction of the tea lady. Ignoring his trick, she offered him a cup of tea. 'One lump or two?' was all she asked.

'No . . . I don't take any,' replied a crestfallen Williams.

'You ain't got any, either, love,' and she ambled off down the corridor, leaving an open-mouthed Williams without a suitable riposte for

perhaps the first time in his entire career.

Camber Sands was the exotic location for *Carry On, Follow That Camel*, and one scene saw both Peter Butterworth and Jim Dale buried up to their necks in sand in the heat of the desert. Although the effect had been achieved by standing the two actors in oil drums beneath ground level, they still had to be buried from the shoulders up to the neck and were genuinely unable to move or dig their way out. Of course, the inevitable happened, orchestrated by visiting American comedy star Phil Silvers. As soon as the take they were working on was over, a tea break was called. The entire cast and crew headed off towards the refreshments tent a quarter of a mile away, leaving Dale and Butterworth still buried up to their necks. Their loud protests quickly turned from mild amusement to total despair and it was quite some time before Silvers returned with a couple of technicians to dig them out.

Dale and Butterworth managed to get their own back on Silvers on his birthday. As a rule, Silvers didn't make it a habit to socialise with his co-stars, but he agreed to join them in the hotel bar at Camber Sands so they could wish him a happy birthday with a toast.

After one drink, Silvers retreated to his suite, claiming he was unwell and had a migraine. Dale and Butterworth quickly went to work and got a blank bill from one of the waiters. They spent some time neatly writing out an endless list of expensive drinks on it, adding up to an impressive total at the end. The icing on the cake was to write a charming letter from the cast to Silvers, thanking him for being so generous in buying them so many rounds on the occasion of his birthday. The bill and letter were delivered to Silvers' bedroom. Butterworth and Dale had lit the blue touchpaper. They then retreated to watch the resulting fireworks.

For a man who had been so poorly earlier on in the evening, Silvers wasted no time in jumping out of bed and locating the hotel manager. During his discussion with the manager, his voice rose to a level quite extraordinary for a man professing to have a migraine. When the truth came out, Silvers apparently promised personally to bury those two actors

Scott and Williams at their hilarious best in *Carry On Henry*

759-46.

in the sand at his earliest opportunity, only this time he wouldn't stop at the neck!

These kind of stories are endless. Although the conditions the actors had to work under were sometimes horrendous, there was always a sense of fun on the set and, despite the fact that many of the regular cast always replied with the answer 'it was just a job', when asked what it was like to be in a *Carry On* film, there was clearly more than just laughs along the way. There was also friendship, loyalty and commitment to the films and to each other. But where did it all start?

The answer to that can only be found by delving back some forty years to when a partnership between producer Peter Rogers and director Gerald Thomas was formed. The first script they planned to film was about a ballet dancer and her fiancé who was called up to do national service on the day they were due to

Joker Phil Silvers in *Carry On Follow That Camel*

get married. In this lay the beginnings of the *Carry On* phenomenon.

Peter Rogers and Gerald Thomas as two naughty schoolboys

Chapter 2
Let the Naughtiness Begin

'Oh, I say! An Arab, eh? I've heard they're very intense lovers!'
'Well, naturally. They do everything in tents.'
Charles Hawtrey and Sid James, *Carry On Cleo* (1964)

If a criminal had to stand up in court to explain to the jury exactly what the roles of a film producer and a film director were, he'd explain that the producer's job was to get the cash for the film while the director's job was to tell the accomplices how to do it.

One producer, who shall remain anonymous, once admitted that he saw his job in the film industry as being a bit like a criminal mastermind. When asked to explain himself he replied that at the end of the day the motivation of both was exactly the same: both parties had to try to work out different ways of getting money out of the general public's pockets.

When a movie is made, partnerships are often formed. Some manage to endure, with the producer and director working together on many subsequent movies, while other relationships fall apart as soon as the film is loaded into the camera. Peter Rogers and Gerald Thomas were an extraordinarily successful duo, so much so that they are probably the most

Gerald Thomas relaxes at home with his family in 1969

21

lasting partnership that the British film industry is ever likely to see - but there was more to their relationship than just the 31 *Carry On* films they made together. They were good friends both on and off the film sets.

Although most contemporary critics derided their work, there was no denying that they were financially successful. Rogers and Thomas could produce what the public loved and wanted to see at the cinema. On one occasion, a brash interviewer cornered Peter Rogers at the Pinewood film studios in Buckinghamshire.

'Still making the same old crap, Peter?' he asked.

'If you call money crap, then yes I am,' Rogers replied.

Before they teamed up for the *Carry On* series, both Rogers and Thomas had had many years of experience in the film industry, and they knew each other well. Thomas's brother, Ralph, had been a successful film director and it was during a break in filming a World War II epic called *Above Us the Waves* that Gerald, who was working as a film editor at the time, met Peter Rogers. Both men got along so well that they decided to form a film production partnership.

This was in 1955. In the previous year Ralph had worked alongside Roger's wife, the renowned producer Betty Box, on a huge box-office success called *Doctor in the House*. This had been the first in a long-running series of films they went on to make, based on the semi-autobiographical books by Richard Gordon. There was obviously a case for keeping partnerships in the family!

Rogers had some experience as an associate producer to his credit and he was also a skilled scriptwriter. He was soon developing projects that he could work on with Gerald Thomas. At first, they experienced setbacks as none of the major distributors or backers were willing to finance any of their ideas. Without money, it was impossible to get their first feature off the ground.

A year of frustration eventually came to an end when the Children's Film Foundation stepped in with enough money to finance Circus Friends, which Rogers wrote and produced while Thomas called the shots from behind the camera. The film eventually made it to the big screen in 1956 and at last, Rogers and Thomas were on their way.

In the following year they took out an option on the rights of a play, *Time Lock*, by Arthur Hailey, author of the successful novel *Airport* which had already been made into a mini-series in Canada. *Time Lock* gave Rogers and Thomas their first taste of critical success; critics hailing the film as a masterful thriller which revolved around a father's struggle to free his son from a bank vault he was trapped in.

Having achieved a degree of recognition, Rogers and Thomas then thought they would turn their talents to something more lightweight, and tackled a project called *The Duke Wore Jeans*, which was a musical vehicle for the immensely popular Tommy Steele. It was while working on this that Rogers acquired the rights to *The Bull Boys*, a script that the popular English novelist R. F. Delderfield had written. Sidney Box, Rogers' brother-in-law, had tried to get the project on screen but had given up. He happily passed it on to Rogers. *The Bull*

COME UNTO US ALL YOU WHO ARE HEAVY LADEN

Boys was a relatively simple plot revolving around a pair of ballet dancers falling in love, only to have their marriage plans foiled when the man is called up for two years of national service, much to his fiancée's frustration.

Rogers liked the plot but wanted to rework it into a more lighthearted comedy. He hunted around for someone to redraft the material and first chose Eric Sykes. At the time Sykes was out of love with the film industry, having been badly treated by a film producer only weeks before Rogers' approach. He told Rogers what he thought of his offer in no uncertain terms and showed him the door.

Rogers tried the same door again. Sykes was based at an office run by Beryl Vertue,

Thomas and Rogers joined the cast for a photo call after the wedding scene in *Carry On Again Doctor*

which was a hive of activity in all things comic, as it housed such major talents as Eric Sykes, Ray Galton and Alan Simpson, the legendary writing partnership of *Hancock's Half Hour* and *Steptoe and Son*. Rogers' second choice was Spike Milligan. He went to see him in the same building he saw Sykes. There, he found Milligan sitting behind his desk with a loaded revolver in his hands. This, Milligan explained, was going to be used to kill his wife! Rogers suggested divorce as a less dramatic option and beat a hasty retreat to John Antrobus's office, which too was in the same building. Antrobus happily agreed to take on the rewrite and broaden its comic potential.

Next, Rogers set about choosing a producer for the project. Gerald Thomas, surprisingly, was not his first choice. He gave first refusal to Muriel Box, his sister-in-law who had such films as *The Beachcomber* and *Eyewitness* to her credit, but she turned him down. Second on his list was Val Guest, who had handled the first major hit that Hammer Films enjoyed with *The Quatermass Experiment*. He too turned Rogers down. It was a case of third time lucky. Rogers turned to the director he had under contract, and Gerald Thomas was more than happy to direct the film.

By the time Rogers found his producer, Antrobus had completed his work on *The Bull Boys*. Even though the improvements were dramatic, Rogers still felt that it wasn't quite right and looked for someone who could tighten the script further still. His eyes rested on Norman Hudis. Norman Hudis was still under contract to Rogers, having worked with him on *The Duke Wore Jeans*. Although he generally worked on more dramatic scripts, he set about reworking *The Bull Boys*, introducing some radical restructuring to the plot.

Financing came next, with Rogers securing a deal with Stuart Levy and Nat Cohen, who ran one of the major film distribution companies in England called Anglo-Amalgamated. It was during one of their initial financial meetings together that Levy suggested a title change for the project. He felt certain that *The Bull Boys* would be box-office poison, and felt something far more lighthearted was needed. *Carry On Sergeant*

seemed like the obvious choice. A film entitled *Carry On Admiral* had been released in the previous year and had made a fair return on its production costs at the box-office. Levy saw no reason why Rogers couldn't cash in on that film's success and use the 'Carry On' prefix on his project.

If Levy hadn't come up with that idea, then

in all probability there would never have been any other *Carry On* films other than *Carry On Admiral*, which is always confused as being part of the official *Carry On* series. Nobody could have foreseen how vast an impact the finished product would have and how the title *Carry On Sergeant* would become part of English culture.

Sir Malcolm Sergeant would read banners proclaiming 'Carry On Sergeant' at the annual proms concerts he conducted and Rogers recalls an incident at the premiere of a film starring Laurence Olivier where the

Charles Hawtrey gets an earful in *Carry On Sergeant*

simple line, 'Carry on, Sergeant,' reduced the audience into hysterics during a dramatic scene.

After the success of *Carry On Sergeant* things were never quite the same again for Rogers and Thomas. With a budget of just £74,000 and a mere six-week shooting schedule, they began filming on 24 March 1958, mixing location work at the Queen's Barracks in Guildford, Surrey, with studio sequences at Pinewood.

Playing the sergeant of the film's title was William Hartnell, who later went on to become the first Doctor Who. He was as abrupt and aggressive off-screen as he was on, and was the ideal character to bring Sergeant Grimshaw to life. The logic of casting him was simple; he had played a similar character to great acclaim in the long-running television sitcom, *The Army Game.*

He did, unfortunately, behave like a real sergeant towards the cast playing his troops. It was very bad news for any actor who fluffed his lines and spoiled the take; Hartnell would snarl at him through gritted teeth, calling him all sorts of names when such delays kept him away from his tea breaks. Hartnell kept his 'troops' in line and thoroughly drilled, and even managed, on one occasion, to fool the top brass.

A visiting Brigadier witnessed a sequence being filmed which entailed Hartnell making his men pound the tarmac of the drill square. The camera crew was hidden from view with the result that the Brigadier was convinced he was witnessing a real drill. At the end of the sequence he went over to Hartnell and praised him, making it quite clear that he thought his soldiers displayed

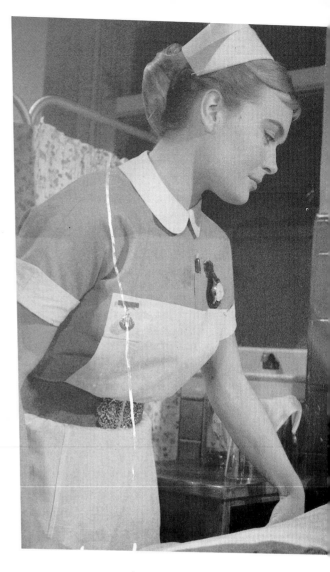

the kind of pride in appearance and drill skills that all soldiers should strive for. And he wasn't finished when the truth was pointed out to him. A few days following the incident a formal letter arrived at the barracks, saying that if any of the actors wanted to join the army, the Brigadier was certain he could find them the right places!

Both Bob Monkhouse and Kenneth Williams credited the success of their drill performance to Hartnell's barking of orders, while Kenneth Connor has a similar memory

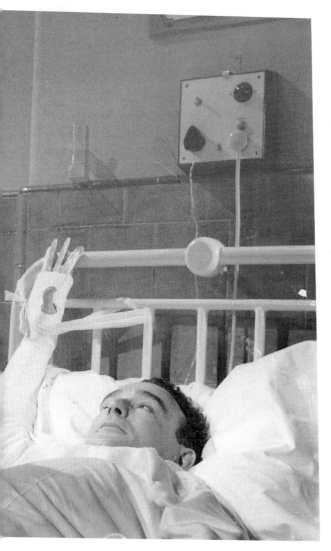

Shirley Eaton tends to Kenneth Connor in
Carry On Nurse

of the film:

'Hartnell was not someone you would want to be seen messing around in front of. People were quite edgy when he was around. He'd been in the business since the year dot and anything that wasn't seen by him as being the height of professionalism was tantermount to treason. I'm certain he would have had some of us out on that tarmac in front of a firing squad if he'd been given half a chance. As far as making the film was concerned, what you saw on screen was what you got off screen as well ... He was frightening!'

As filming progressed the antics increased; at the barracks the actors took great pleasure in wandering around the camp between filming sessions looking as slovenly as possible, with hands in pockets and berets at impossible angles. Inevitably they were bellowed at by all passing officers and took great pleasure in pointing out that they were merely actors from the film unit. After a while the real soldiers picked up on this trick and because the officers didn't want to get caught reprimanding actors again, there was a relatively scruffy-looking soldiery in the Guildford barracks for a few weeks, for the officers couldn't tell the real thing from the actors!

One incident took place during the filming of the assault course sequence, where many of the characters were seen swinging on a rope across a water-filled muddy pit. After Charles Hawtrey had successfully completed his scene, falling on to his backside in the slime, it came to Bob Monkhouse's turn on the rope. Nobody, however, had noticed what Kenneth Williams had been up to while the cameras were filming Hawtrey in the mud.

Due to the pound and a half of butter that Williams had smeared all over the rope, no matter how frantically Monkhouse gripped it, he found himself sliding downwards into the watery hole Hawtrey had just clambered out of. This wasn't part of the script. Howling with laughter, Williams taunted Monkhouse by calling him 'Mudhouse'. Even Monkhouse had to join in with the laughter.

Of all the actors who appeared in the *Carry On* series, Williams was the most notorious practical joker. As he freely admitted in an interview he gave in 1982: 'I can't see anything wrong with a little harmless fun ... especially if it's the harmless you are making fun of!'

The daily rushes of sequences were quickly sent to London so the distributors could see what was being shot as the days progressed. Rogers soon found out that they were far from being happy. The unedited sequences hardly raised a smile, let alone a laugh amongst the distributors, and Rogers had to explain that the comedy would come in the editing, when Thomas strung the sequences together in the correct order to make the humour shine through. This did little to placate them and Rogers vowed that it would be the last time he would ever allow any *Carry On* rushes to be seen during filming.

The distributors' worries were, of course, unfounded. The box-office reaction to *Carry On Sergeant* was as immediate as it was immense. Crowds flocked to the cinema to see the film, and as a result of their enthusiasm, *Sergeant* became the third top grossing film at the UK box-office for 1958. Rogers and Thomas had a hit on their hands and their financial backers, Levy and Cohen, wanted a follow-up - and fast. Rogers and Thomas racked their brains for a new idea.

A few years previously, Rogers and his wife had gone to the theatre to see a play called *Ring for Catty*, which had been written by future *Father Dear Father* star Patrick Cargill and Jack Searle. Realising that it had cinematic potential, Rogers had secured the film rights shortly thereafter. After rereading the script he became even more convinced that the material was there for a medical *Carry On* send up. He took this idea to Cohen and Levy.

By the end of the meeting *Carry On Nurse* had obtained the financial backing it needed to get it off the ground and Norman Hudis was quickly contracted as the film's screenwriter. Although *Carry On Nurse* bears no relation to *Ring for Catty*, Rogers still gave the original play's writers a small royalty and a credit on the finished film.

Hudis, however, hit a brick wall as he stared at the blank pages he had to fill. He thought *Nurse* was nowhere near as enjoyable or easy to adapt as *Sergeant* but his viewpoint changed when fate intervened to give him a helping hand. Due to ill health Hudis wound up in hospital for 10 days and took in enough of the action there to fuel his creativity. On his return home he finished the script for *Nurse* in just under a week.

The highlight of the film - or indeed in any *Carry On* film - came about as a result of Hudis talking to his mother-in-law. It was she who told him about the daffodil gag and Hudis interpreted it with Hattie Jacques as Matron and Wilfrid Hyde-White as the helpless colonel lying face-down on the bed. Hyde-White was not actually present when Hattie Jacques's reaction shots were being filmed and he later threatened to sue Rogers for misrepresenting his rear on screen, claiming he had no knowledge of what the director and the producer were planning to do. He subsequently dropped the threats when he realised that no court on earth would have heard his complaint with a straight face.

Jacques herself suffered above and beyond the call of duty filming that scene, for when she reached out to pull the daffodil free (the stem was off camera!), some joker put a finger into their mouth and popped their cheek to sound like a champagne cork going off right on cue. Jacques nearly collapsed with laughter as did the crew, and after an afternoon of attempted retakes, the shot had to be abandoned until the following morning. Only after a night's sleep did the cast and crew sufficiently recover their composure to be able to continue filming.

Six weeks of filming *Carry On Nurse* at Pinewood began on 3 November 1958. On that date Rogers told the press that at least four more titles would follow in the series, with *Teacher*, *Constable*, *Regardless* and *What a Carry On* coming next. The final title on his list never made it and now no one can remember what *What a Carry On* was going to be about.

Many actors found filming Carry On Nurse a strange experience, due to the fact that their day involved getting up out of bed, travelling to Pinewood and then getting back into bed again! As Kenneth Connor recalls: 'We were like zombies. The nights at home were restless because you'd have been in bed all day, and then when you were in the studio, the heat from the arc lamps had the effect of a sedative so you slowly nodded off. It's quite true to say that I was caught on more than one occasion by the sound engineers, because my snoring was interfering with their microphones.'

Connor as Gregory Adams in *Carry On Teacher*

When confronted with the accusation that he too had fallen asleep, an indignant Kenneth Williams exploded with outrage at the very suggestion that he was capable of such a thing. He was caught out, however, when Gerald Thomas arranged for a photographer to come in and be on standby with a camera. When Williams nodded off, the photographer crept up to his bed, put a sign on his chest and took a picture.

Thomas kept quiet about the incident until the next time Williams swore blind he never slept on the job. Gleefully he presented Williams with a photograph of him, fast asleep in bed with a sign around his neck reading, 'Spare a copper for an ex-actor, Guv. Available on HP to careful users'. Williams was lost for words.

No one really expected *Carry On Nurse* to do as well as *Sergeant*. The film industry was governed by the law of diminishing returns, but *Nurse* shattered that particular notion. There was no number three position in the top ten film chart this time because *Carry On Nurse* quickly made it to the top, and became the hit film of 1959.

After the lukewarm reaction at the American box-office with *Carry On Sergeant*, *Nurse* managed to confound expectations in that area as well. This was in no small part due to the solo efforts of an independent film distributor, David Emmanuel. His faith in the product was huge and he literally made his way around the country transporting the prints of the film he had himself, showing them at various cinemas and topping off the audiences' enjoyment of the screenings by handing out plastic daffodils at

the end. A cult following quickly spread throughout the country and each showing was a sell out based on word of mouth alone.

Back in England, Hudis was already at work on the script of *Carry On Teacher*. Gerald Thomas had just completed work on a comedy called *Please Turn Over* which Hudis had adapted for the screen from a play which had been a huge hit in London's West End. The leading star in this play had been an actor called Ted Ray. Ray was then a huge star due to his radio show, *Ray's A Laugh*, and he made numerous appearances in various television shows. He seemed a natural to bring into the *Carry On* team and Thomas asked Hudis to write *Carry On Teacher* with Ray in mind. The result was the character of William Wakefield.

Location filming began for the inevitable six weeks shooting period on 9 March 1959, at Drayton Secondary School in West Ealing, London. A routine was gradually establishing itself for the *Carry Ons*; two films would be made a year with shooting taking place in the spring and autumn. This was simply to avoid losing any members of the regular team who had commitments in

shows either throughout the summer season or winter pantomime.

When *Teacher* moved into Pinewood, where the sets for the classroom interiors had been erected, Kenneth Williams struck again, his target this time being Kenneth Connor. One sequence involved Connor's character, science teacher Gregory Adams, examining the contents of a glass jar in the school's laboratory. The rehearsals went fine but when it came to the first take and the lid was removed from the jar, Connor nearly passed out. Williams had emptied the contents of a packet of stink bombs into it, and Connor had just taken a huge sniff. He did, however, get his own back on Williams, as he recalls: 'There's a scene in *Carry On Teacher* where the children have covered our clothes with itching powder, but in truth Kenneth was the only one with the real thing in his jacket due to a ten bob note exchanging between me and one of the wardrobe girls. I'm certain he knew exactly what had happened but he never let on. He never allowed you to reveal the fact that you'd got your own back on him.'

Interviewed in 1977, Hattie Jacques added her thoughts on Williams' notorious reputation as a practical joker. 'Kenneth loves his little jokes and can be quite naughty when he's in one of his moods, but he never plays his tricks on me. We go back quite some way [*Hancock's Half Hour* in the 1950s where Williams and Jacques were both part of the series' rep of actors] and he's a bit naughty like a little brother ... so I suppose I'm like his big sister!'

In 1987 Thomas and Rogers announced plans for a 30th Anniversary *Carry On* which never came about

Carry On Teacher was the only outing Ted Ray made with the *Carry On* team and there are indications that this wasn't the original plan. More than one person involved in the series had intimated that Ray would have become a *Carry On* regular if it wasn't for the fact that he was contracted to another production/distribution company who were not keen on seeing him in another company's highly successful film when they had failed to even give him a film to star in in the first place. After Ray's departure Rogers brought in the lesser-known actor, Sid James.

This was not the end of Ray's association with many on the team, because he went on to work with them again on both radio and television. He died in 1977 and in 1978

Kenneth Williams paid this tribute to him: 'Ted has an immense understanding of comedy and the mechanics that are part of its art form; in fact, even more so than many people I worked with before or since. He was a true craftsman and it's a shame he only appeared in one of the *Carry On*s.'

Carry On Teacher was another big hit on

Hattie Jacques as Sergeant Laura Moon

both sides of the Atlantic, and there was now a demand for the next film to be ready for release before Christmas 1959. With the budget for production hovering between

£70,000 and £80,000, the initial three films were more than making their costs back and in so doing, they were practically guaranteeing that there was more than enough money to make the next film in the series: *Carry On*

Constable* was Sid James' first *Carry On

Williams and Hawtrey go shopping

Constable.

There really should have been a warning issued to the general public before shooting began, drawing attention to the fact that the *Carry On* team had been let loose in the streets of Ealing in police uniforms. As usual, it was Kenneth Williams who inevitably led the way when the chaos started.

Sid James living it up in the *Carry On Long John* 1970 Christmas TV special

It was just too much of an opportunity to miss and Williams and Leslie Philips were soon standing in the middle of the main road running through the area, redirecting traffic and causing minor traffic jams in the process. Not one of the bemused motorists either questioned them or recognised who they were, and they somehow managed to get the flow of traffic back in order before real officers of the law arrived at the scene of the crime.

Inevitably, when people stopped to ask Williams for directions, his total unfamiliarity with the area didn't stop him from sending them off wherever he saw fit, and during one sequence where his character has to show a

reluctant old lady across the road, a real OAP who witnessed this stopped and asked him to show her across as well. A round of applause greeted his return from the opposite side of the road, after he'd stopped filming to be able to carry out the old lady's request.

The real police also ended up getting involved in the action during the location shoot, all because of a case of mistaken identity. In the film's storyline Williams and Hawtrey have to go undercover in a department store wearing drag in order to capture some shoplifters redhanded. Through their own incompetence they end up being mistaken for shoplifters themselves and are pursued through the streets by the store's assistant manager. During the first take on this sequence, a real officer saw the chase and joined in, convinced that a real crime was in progress. He was extremely embarrassed when told what was really going on.

Carry On Constable was the film which introduced Sid James as part of the regular *Carry On* team. He told the press he was very happy to be part of 'Rogers and Thomas's happy family' but that didn't stop an unrelenting prank being played on him at every opportunity. Someone was filling his boots with sand; it was never enough to stop him being able to put the footwear on but just enough to grind the skin off his heels. It got to be so bad that James would take his policeman's boots home with him every evening to stop the sabotage. Nobody owned up to this particular trick but it was more than likely that Kenneth Williams was somehow involved.

Like Hawtrey and Connor, Williams was delighted by the fact that the *Carry On* films were now becoming a regular event. It was nice to have the security of knowing that every four months a script would

arrive and that there were usually two films to make a year. Recalling the situation in 1982 he said: 'It came to a point where you could almost set your watch by the arrival of a *Carry On* script. It was as regular as clockwork. It was always a pleasure to remind yourself when you were stuck in an awful revue or something, that there was always a *Carry On* waiting just around the corner to relieve the tedium, and part of the fun was the fact that you never knew what Gerald Thomas would be asking you to do next.'

The title of the next film seemed to sum up Williams' attitude perfectly. *Carry On Regardless* must have come as a surprise to Williams, and it would have most certainly relieved any symptoms of boredom, for in this film he was required to play an escort ... to a chimpanzee! When Thomas took Williams out on to the streets of Windsor in December 1960, his co-star was a youngster by the name of Yoki, and part of the action involved Williams joining in with a chimp's

35

Kenneth Connor forlornly expected an exotic location for *Carry On Cruising*

again, leaving Williams lost for words - and breath.

It was in the early 1960s that talks began about moving the films into the world of technicolour; the profits on the initial films were so good that budgets on the films in production were getting bigger; *Regardless* had a budget nudging the £100,000 mark. The script on this film too was more adventurous than in the previous ones; Hudis's approach was to give a series of sketches and comedy sequences a linking theme, using Bert's Handy Agency as the central base on which all the action revolves.

One of the sketches involved Joan Sims' character slowly getting plastered at a wine tasting evening. During that scene there is no fake alcohol on view at all and every glass she drank during the shooting of that sequence is a glass of the real thing. Normally a supply of cold tea and coloured water is used as an alcohol substitute but

tea party. Everything went well while the cameras were rolling, with all the chimps behaving perfectly. Williams had initially expressed reluctance at actually being so near to so many animals at once, but he soon settled down and began to enjoy himself. Once the scene was completed to Thomas's satisfaction, Williams strode up to one of the prop men and commented that his opinion of apes had changed and he now thought them to be one of the most well-mannered and charming of animals. As if on cue, one of the said creatures charged up to the actor, hit him in the groin and ran off

Thomas couldn't resist the chance of getting real reaction shots of Sims. Hence when she swigs down some clear liquid and turns pale on screen, there's very little acting involved because Thomas had made sure her glass was overflowing with neat gin. By the end of that shooting session it would be no exaggeration to say Sims was in a thoroughly pickled state!

Shooting finished on *Regardless* towards the end of January 1961, and although there would be a break of close to nine months before work on the next *Carry On* would begin, Rogers and Thomas were far from being idle. The man behind the music on all of the films to date, Bruce Montgomery, had come up with a story about a young student of classical music who dreams up a pop song and quite literally rocks the establishment he's at. *Raising the Wind* was drafted and scheduled to go before the cameras during the following few months, alongside another Rogers and Thomas venture called *Watch Your Stern*. Both films starred many of the *Carry On* regulars - Sid James, Liz Fraser, Leslie Philips and Kenneth Williams appearing in Montgomery's story, and Kenneth Connor, Joan Sims, Hattie Jacques and Leslie Philips again appearing in *Watch Your Stern*.

Hawtrey agitated for star billing and was dumped on

Another actor present in both these films was Eric Barker, who like Montgomery, took the opportunity to pitch an idea to the ever-receptive Rogers while the naval antics of *Watch Your Stern* were underway. His suggestion was to set a *Carry On* adventure around a holiday cruise, using the regular cast as the crew. Rogers gave him a commission to work on a storyline for the project.

One of the supporting cast members of *Raising the Wind* was a pop star of the late 1950s, Jim Dale, who was now building an acting career. Spotting the potential Dale had as a comedian, it was actually Kenneth Williams who went

to Thomas and suggested that Dale be drafted in as one of the regulars of the *Carry On* team.

Rogers enlisted Hudis to work on Barker's finished plotline to turn it into another *Carry On*. Hudis had actually been busy working on yet another film based on Cargil and Searle's play *Ring for Catty*, with Rogers this time wanting a direct adaptation of the script. Retitled as *Twice Around the Daffodils* as an in-joke, the project would not go before the cameras until Barker's new idea, now titled *Carry On Cruising* had been finished. There was huge excitement over *Carry On Cruising*. With the enormous budget of £140,000 allocated to it, it marked the first time that a *Carry On* would be filmed in colour. When word started to spread among the regulars that the new film centred around an ocean cruiseliner, images started to fill the team's minds of breaking free of the confines of Pinewood at last. Perhaps they would film in China or Hong Kong, or some exotic location in the West Indies. Kenneth Connor was certainly fooled, as he recalls: 'We were told words to the effect that yes, we would be on an ocean liner for the duration of filming, and it was only Kenny Williams who was really suspicious. You see, although Peter Rogers is a wonderful man to work for, expenses for exotic locations are not something that he can cope with. It would mean spending money! I thought we'd at least get to the Mediterranean but Kenny [Williams] reckoned we'd get only as far as Glasgow!'

Many of the cast still believed that there was no way they'd end up in Pinewood with broken glass floating in water with a light aimed at it to make it look as though the sea was being reflected on the set, but that's exactly what happened, and even though the set for the liner was vast and impressive, it was no substitute for the real thing. There was talk of of filming some sequences on a real ship, but as Williams may have predicted, it was planned to be in a salvage dock. In the end this came to nothing.

One star who was absent from *Cruising* was Charles Hawtrey. The role that Hudis had created for him as the ship's chef was given instead to Lance Percival, a regular of *That Was The Week That Was*. The reason for Hawtrey's absence was complicated but it involved star billing. The stars of the film were Williams and James but Hawtrey was badgering Rogers for his name to be put over theirs. Rogers wasn't going to agree to do this and in a fit of pique Hawtrey complained that he didn't have a silver star on the door of his dressing room with his name emblazoned across it. Hawtrey didn't appear in *Cruising* but differences were ironed out before the next film. In fact, Hawtrey would appear in every subsequent *Carry On* until *Carry On Camping* in 1972, where the reasons for his departure for the second and final time were just as complex.

At this point in time Williams too was growing disenchanted with the *Carry On* films, noting that many of the original actors who had been in *Sergeant* had now left the series, and only Connor and he remained. He therefore took a year's leave of absence, although he is on view in *Twice Round the Daffodils* which started filming just as soon as *Cruising* was finished.

Twice Around the Daffodils marked the end of Hudis's scriptwriting for Rogers and Thomas. He had completed in total six

Sid James on his way to the bookies

Carry On scripts and wanted to move on to pastures new. His departure to America coincided with the release of *Cruising*.

Other writers would now have to be found to fill his shoes. One candidate, Michael Pertwee, suggested making a *Carry On* based around a fire station. *Carry On Smoking* would have been tailored for Sid James as the Fire Chief while Williams and Hawtrey would have been offered support roles. Rogers was unconvinced, fearing he would have to pull such a film from release if there was a major disaster or accident at the time of the première. He was also reluctant to commit to such a project as a similar film had been released in 1961, *Go To Blazes*,

starring Dave King and Robert Morley. *Carry On Smoking* was extinguished before it had ever really had the chance to spark into life.

In fact, their new writer was already working for them. After completing a film called *The Iron Maiden*, Rogers and Thomas were due to begin work on a project called Call Me a Cab, which a writer by the name of Talbot Rothwell had scripted. James, Jacques, Connor and Hawtrey had already been cast so Rogers and Thomas did the natural thing. They turned *Call Me a Cab* into *Carry On Cabby*.

James and Jacques in *Carry On Cabby*

Chapter 3
Tittering in the Aisles

'And may his radiance light up your life.'
'And up yours.'
Kenneth Williams and Sid James, *Carry On Up the Khyber* (1968)

'It doesn't matter if you are the most talented, gifted of actors that there's ever been, because when some people try to be funny on cue, they simply die! I have no idea how to explain what the secret of comedy is. I just don't know, and I don't think I'd ever want to know the answer, to be honest. I just learn my lines, turn up on set and play it straight. So far, so good - it seems to be paying off. It's as simple as that.'

Sid James's candid remarks during the making of *Carry On Cabby* are actually quite revealing. This was a man who didn't suffer fools gladly, and just wanted to get on with the job in hand. If there was one thing that filled him with dread more than anything else, it was the thought of having to ad-lib. He just couldn't do it - and if it wasn't scripted, then he wouldn't do it.

In his *Diaries* Kenneth Williams recalled that he and James had rows on more than one occasion during the course of making the *Carry On* films, and this was due entirely to Williams' antics both on and off camera. James found such behaviour very difficult to deal with, but with Hattie Jacques, his on-screen wife for *Cabby*, he couldn't have wished for a better acting partner. All his

memories of her were full of praise and affection.

'Hattie knows exactly what she's doing. She can say so much with one of her looks, and really knows how to bring grace to any part she plays. There have been some instances in the past when one or two people have failed to see her potential, but that's not the case at all with the *Carry On* people. They adore her, and I couldn't agree with them more.'

James's reference to 'the past' was probably a dig at *Hancock's Half Hour* where both he and Jacques fell foul of Hancock's desire to work alone, and the two of them, together with Kenneth Williams, eventually found that their services were no longer required. All in all, the atmosphere on the *Carry On* films was far more relaxed and happier than on the *Hancock* series.

Carry On Cabby gave Jacques her favourite role in any of the fourteen films of the series she appeared in. Speaking in 1977, she commented: 'Peggy was a favourite of mine, even over the times that I played Matron. She was strong inside, and really decided to fight back against the fact that her husband was ignoring her. She had to draw attention to herself to win him back, and the only way to do that was to fight him at his own game. That's why I liked her. She wasn't someone who was prepared to sit on the sidelines anymore.'

The winding country lanes and small towns of Buckinghamshire near the Pinewood studios formed the main location sites for *Carry On Cabby*, when filming began in March 1963. Its original title of *Call Me a Cab* only changed after shooting had been completed. *Carry On Cabby* marked the debut in the series of Jim Dale as an anxious father whose wife is about to give birth at any moment. His single day's work on the film was one of the last to be shot.

The tradition of featuring a drag sequence in the films continued in *Cabby*, and this time it was Kenneth Connor's turn to don the wig and suspenders. It was something he carried out without much joy, he remembers: 'The whole gag with the *Carry On* drag routines was that they always made sure that it was either patently ridiculous or rather convincing. I hated it, and I know that Sid [James] was not that fond of the times he had to wear a dress. On the other hand, Charles Hawtrey loved it, but the problem with that was that he did make a very convincing matronly figure but it was just

Jim Dale in
Carry On Jack

so obvious that it was him. There was no way that you could ever look at him and keep a straight face when he was dressed like that. But then again, I don't think I would have ever qualified as a Miss World contestant!'

Prior to *Cabby*, James had actually starred in a long-running BBC sitcom called *Taxi*, and as on the television series set, he would occasionally drive off during lunch breaks in the cab allotted to him. He said he did this because it gave him a great sense of anonymity, but everyone knew that the vehicle could easily be found outside the nearest betting shop in the area where filming was taking place. As someone once observed, with the amount of mileage that James got out of his cab, he probably qualified for passing 'the knowledge' without even realising it!

Talbot Rothwell had, in Peter Rogers and Gerald Thomas, found a production partnership that was perfectly in tune with his style of writing and humour. His background in the field of comedy was faultless; he had written material for the likes of Terry-Thomas, Arthur Askey and the Crazy Gang, led by Bud Flanagan and Chesney Allen. He had also penned a number of hugely successful West End plays. His pedigree was perfect and he proved to be the ideal replacement for Norman Hudis.

Rogers and Thomas were therefore eager to see a script that Rothwell had completed called *Up the Armada*, which immediately struck them as being perfect material to turn into the next *Carry On* film. 1962 had been the year of the revival of *Mutiny on the Bounty*, when a new version of the film starring Marlon Brando and Trevor Howard was released. The film had been very successful and was the ideal target for a parody. *Up the Armada* was certainly sending up the whole naval genre, with scenes of plank walking and flogging, but Rogers and Thomas soon found they ran into problems over the title.

Although in the past there had been no serious problems with the censors, the *Carry On* team had been tweaked now and then; there had been concern over how the name of Allcock would be pronounced in *Teacher*

Juliet Mills before being press ganged

while a line from *Carry On Nurse* also excited the censors. In a scene where a patient's lead weights supporting his broken leg fall to the ground, Matron asks someone to pick up his balls. The censors were not happy about that line but let it stay; however they were not prepared to compromise over *Carry On Up the Armada*. They felt that the title passed the line of risque and entered the realm of the blatantly rude, so it had to change. As sailors were nicknamed 'jolly jack-tars' during the eighteenth century, a substitute of *Carry On Jack* was quickly devised and the decision to film in colour was made. It's interesting to note that for a brief period, the very obvious title that could have been used, *Carry On Sailor*, was under consideration, but was dropped during the course of filming.

Once again, any hopes that the cast may have had about working in a hot foreign country soon went out the window when location scenes started to be staged in the first few weeks of September 1963. The closest cast and crew got to a tropical paradise was Frensham Ponds in the heart of Surrey. This site had been used in the past for all manner of different locations, and on *Jack* all the land and water scenes were filmed there while scenes from the ship's interiors and deck were rigged up in the confines of Pinewood Studios.

The tone of *Carry On Jack* was darker than that of the previous *Carry On*s, with scenes of potential violence which needed careful handling on the part of Thomas to avoid more trouble with the censors. On one of the filming days, Hawtrey spent an afternoon looking like a bomb-blast victim, with his clothes in shreds, his face black with soot and his hair standing on end because his character, Walter Sweetley, had been caught in the backdraft of an exploding cannon. Hawtrey, who was dying for a smoke, wisely left the set to have a cigarette, wishing to avoid setting off any explosions with burning ash. Discovering that he didn't have his lighter or matches with him, he failed to see the joke when people burst into hysterical laughter every time he approached them and asked them for a light. He was heard to say, 'All I want to do is have a bloody smoke!' which led to even more laughter, before he finally stormed off in a temper.

Carry On Jack was the first of the major historical hystericals that Rogers and Thomas made under the *Carry On* banner, and they tended to be the most popular ones with many of the cast. When asked why he thought this was by a journalist, Williams replied: 'It's like playing Cowboys and Indians when you were young. There's a side to everyone that still longs to be able to do that kind of thing, and it's only actors who can dress up outrageously, act

outrageously, and still get away with it. And, of course, the icing on the cake is that we get paid for it as well!'

By this time, the general public were becoming increasingly eager to help come up with ideas that the *Carry On* films should take on, and Rogers was receiving suggestions by the sackful, ranging from *Carry On Waltzing* (covering a ballroom dancing competition) to *Carry On Monster Making* (a Frankenstein send up). None of these ideas were taken up.

One or two of the regular cast were also coming up with their own ideas, which were duly pitched to Rogers who listened to what they had to say. *Carry On Cruising* came about because he listened to Eric Barker, but he didn't pursue Jim Dale's idea of *Carry On Camelot* or Charles Hawtrey's rather strange idea of parodying the plays of Oscar Wilde.

Joining forces with the highly respected

television writer Sid Colin, Rothwell focused his attention on the spy movie genre which was booming in the early 1960s, due mainly to the arrival of secret agent 007 to the big screen. With *Carry On Jack* out on general

ever, filming was carried out at Pinewood and news soon spread on the grapevine that Charles Hawtrey would be playing a character called James Bind, ranked as secret agent 001 1/2. Faster than a speeding bullet, the Bond producers were on the phone to Rogers.

Rogers conceded that using the '00' tag may have been a bit close to their franchise but he remained firm on using the Bind name. It stayed, and Hawtrey played the character, although in retrospect he may have wished he had never agreed to appear in the film in the first place. At the climax of the story Hawtrey, Williams, Bernard Cribbins and Barbara Windsor are put through a series of various devices along a conveyor belt as Dr Crow, the evil master-

Swashbuckling adventure on the high seas - actually Frensham Ponds

release in early 1964, shooting for *Carry On Spying* began in February of that year. As

mind behind the STENCH organisation, tries to destroy them. It seems that the ordeal was a far from pleasant experience and it looks on film as if Hawtrey is the only one

Bernard Cribbins examines Charles Hawtrey's credentials in *Carry On Spying*

who is taking it all in his stride. It soon becomes quite clear as to why this was - he had passed out with nerves as soon as filming the scene had begun!

It was in this film that Barbara Windsor made her debut. At first Rogers and Thomas were concerned about how she would get on with Williams, who was renowned for tormenting newcomers with his acidic wit and outrageous tricks. They needn't have worried. During Williams and Windsor's first scene together where Williams had to pretend to be a master of disguise while wearing a patently obvious false beard, Windsor kept fluffing her lines on the first few takes. Williams soon lost his patience and let rip with some cutting remark that totally outraged her. Pulling herself up to

her full height, she pointed an accusing finger at him and said at the top of her voice: 'Don't shout at me with someone's minge hair hanging off your face, because I won't bloody stand for it!'

Williams was delighted by this and promptly asked Thomas whether they could keep her as part of the team. Windsor and Williams became firm friends from that day onwards, to the extent that when Windsor went on honeymoon after *Carry On Spying* had been completed, Williams went with her and her new husband Ronnie Knight ... taking his mother and sister on the trip as well! The reason Williams always gave as to why he went was simple. He said he had asked Windsor how long she had been going out with Knight, and when she admitted that it had been years, Williams quipped that there would hardly be any great revelations on their wedding night, so he promptly booked plane tickets to go with them.

For *Carry On Spying*, Williams decided to recreate his 'Snide' character from his time on *Hancock's Half Hour*. His part of Desmond Simpkins was played with overt enthusiasm and when years later he was asked about the film, he explained why he had brought Snide out of retirement: 'I'd used Snide once or twice on the television episodes I did of *Hancock* but I never really tried to flesh him out, so *Carry On Spying* seemed like an ideal way to have a go at it. One or two "stop messing abouts" were thrown in for good measure, just to confirm that it was him to the people in the audience who got the joke. Once was enough though. He won't be seen on screen again.'

Rothwell was actively involved in giving interviews to help publicise the film, and made it quite clear at the time that his targets really were James Bond and all his friends and enemies. 'When superspies like James Bond are seen walking across the room in their immaculate suits with their

Spying was Barbara Windsor's first Carry On

immaculate guns and remarkable aim, I like to think that there are other spies several steps behind,' he said, 'ones that aren't good with their guns and who can never quite get the crease in their trousers straight. Those are the men who deserve their moment of glory, even if they mess up everything in the process, and those are the spies which feature in *Carry On Spying*.'

Rothwell was hard at work on his next script while shooting was underway on *Spying*, and his target this time was one which the public was also well aware of. For over a year, not a week had passed without some headline cropping up in the national press about *Cleopatra*. Twentieth Century-Fox had sunk a major fortune into producing what is now ranked as one of the most expensive films to have ever been made, with a vast recreation of ancient Rome having been painstakingly erected at Pinewood. The film was delayed time and time again due to the illness of the film's leading lady, Elizabeth Taylor, and it genuinely seemed at the time that the film would never be

completed. When it was, its première was a major event. The whole world was aware of *Cleopatra* so Rogers and Thomas set about planning an elaborate parody. The result was Carry *On Cleo*. The ultimate poke in the original film's ribs was when Rogers obtained permission to use the *Cleopatra* sets, which were still standing at Pinewood, for his film. Inevitably, there were lawsuits waiting just around the corner, and from more than one source.

Twentieth Century-Fox were furious when they saw the publicity poster that appeared for *Carry On Cleo* , which was a direct send-up of their own publicity poster. Writs were sent to Rogers and he was forced to withdraw his poster. The most unlikely legal rumblings, however, came from the Marks and Spencer retail chain. In the film, the

Kenneth Williams meets a panel of movie critics

characters played by Jim Dale and Kenneth Connor are auctioned off at a slave market by the traders Marcus and Spencius, and M&S retail objected to this. Rogers quickly explained to the company that it was no more than an affectionate send-up and M&S decided to take no further action against the *Carry On* team after a letter of apology had been sent to them.

Only four months after completing work on *Spying*, in July 1964, Thomas began filming *Cleo*. Due mainly to the magnificent sets, the film looked as if thousands of pounds had been spent on it; the irony being that three *Carry On* films could have been made for the cost of the sets alone in *Cleopatra*.

As many of the costumes were also borrowed from the original film, the actual production costs on *Cleo* were extremely modest.

With tongue planted even further in cheek than normal, one of the touches that Rothwell devised with Thomas was to write a pompous narration which ran over certain sequences in the film, and E. V. H. Emmett was hired as the voice-over.

In the Stone Age Britain scenes, one gag involved Kenneth Connor's character, Hengist Pod, inventing a cart with square wheels. Later on in the film, Pod is seen trying to ride a wooden bicycle with square wheels mounted on the frame. This was a painful experience, as Connor later recalls: 'Every time the wheel clunked around, the saddle seemed to deliberately stab at my private regions, so the expression of pain you see on Pod's face is very real. The whole contraption seemed as though it would fall apart at any second but Gerry [Thomas] could see what was going on and went for more than one take, saying that there was dust on the camera lens. I knew damn well that he was lying through his teeth because he'd always get this glint in his eye and you knew that he was well aware of what was going on. I wouldn't say he was being sadistic but he was clearly finding it hard to keep a straight face.'

Although his *Diaries* tell a different story about his feelings towards the *Carry On* films, Kenneth Williams was always pleasant and full of

Jim Dale is auctioned in *Carry On Cleo*

anecdotes when being interviewed to publicise a film. *Carry On Cleo* was, according to him in 1982, the first time that Thomas and Rogers realised that he was destined to play the greatest character in history: 'Well, I mean, Julius Caesar. It was natural casting when they offered me the role. The facial features dictate that roles of such nobility were made for me, but the wind didn't half blow around one's toga. The chill factor in that studio was quite like the Arctic at times and I remember Charles Hawtrey coming up to me and complaining that his bum was cold. I swear to you that he spent the rest of that film wandering around with thermal knickers on, and who could blame him! He was quite taken with his wig in that film but I thought it looked as though some poor cat had dropped dead on his forehead!'

With perhaps one of Williams' most famous lines coming from *Cleo*: 'Infamy! Infamy! they've all got it in fer me!', it seems a

pity that the actor was not that fond of the historical *Carry On*s. He said in another interview: 'The historical *Carry On*s tend to corrupt things a bit too much for my liking. I mean, if Henry VIII really had been like Sid James, what state would the British

Sid James demands a pay rise from Director Gerald Thomas

monarchy be in today? The greatest humour comes from observations of anything that's founded in reality. That gives the audience something to relate to. I mean, we've all been in hospital, so the medical *Carry On*s have a ring of truth to the comedy, making them more relevant and therefore funnier. I always thought it was a shame that we never got around to the worlds of commerce or sport, because there must surely be ample

scope to get jokes out of there.'

In one of his all-too-rare interviews with the press, Sid James clearly had a different opinion to Williams. 'History is fascinating,' he said, 'and there's a goldmine of things to cover out there, from Bluebeard the pirate to the Spanish Inquisition being open to the *Carry On* treatment. I'm all for it. Films like *Spartacus* give people great value for money because they really offer a different kind of entertainment, so the more *Carry On*s we do like that, the happier I'll be.'

A nine month gap came between *Cleo* and the next *Carry On* venture, but Rothwell kept writing for Rogers and Thomas, producing a script entitled *The Big Job*, which was actually more in the spirit of the 1950s Ealing Comedies than the style he had established with the *Carry On*s. Featuring Sid James, Joan Sims and Jim Dale, the story told of the efforts of a pair of criminals as they try to retrieve the loot they stashed in a tree trunk years ago, only to find that since getting out of prison a police station had been built around the tree.

While *The Big Job* was being shot, Rothwell started drafting the script for *Carry On*

Cowboy, which would be set in the days of the wild west. Filming began in August 1965, but the weather was not good and the first day of filming was entirely lost due to torrential rain. It became a case of keeping fingers crossed for the rest of the shooting period, but only the occasional spot of drizzle hampered the cast and crew from that day onwards. Thomas and Rogers always prided themselves on the fact that all the *Carry On*s were brought in ahead of their six weeks filming schedule, but the rainfall had led to *Carry On Cowboy* running one day late.

As usual, the problem of where to find a suitable site close to hand which could also double as an exotic location reared its ugly head. For *Cowboy*, a western town was needed. Chobham Common in Surrey was deemed as a suitable place while all the scenes that revolved around the Indian reservation were shot within the grounds of Black Park near Pinewood, home to many of the Hammer Horror films' gothic forests.

The sequence involving a chase between a stagecoach and the Red Indians was shot at Chobam. Thomas wanted an authentic feel to the scene so he had to devise a way for the wheels of the coach to spew up a dust trail while the vehicle moved along. The horses were kicking up a certain amount of dust, but it wasn't enough. In the end a prop man was called in to lie on the carriage floor between the feet of Jim Dale and Angela Douglas, holding the carriage door slightly open and trailing a dust gun out of it, which he would fire on cue just as soon as the cameras began to roll.

The facade of the western town was actually built at Pinewood, on one of the

Time for a quick regeneration? Jon Pertwee gasps his last in *Carry On Cowboy*

backlots. Behind the saloons, bank and jail fronts lay an extremely busy English motorway!

Cowboy marked the first appearance of Bernard Bresslaw in a *Carry On* film. He played an enormous Red Indian called Little Heap, and actually underwent a baptism of fire on the *Cowboy* set. Bresslaw was six foot seven inches tall and suffered from the most horrendous vertigo, as he explained: 'I was delighted to get the part, and didn't really take in the fact that there was a scene where Little Heap was seen in a tree, and I mean right at the very top, leaning out from the leaves and firing a rifle at Sid James. Well, I kept my fingers crossed that it wouldn't be too high, but when we got to Black Park, Gerald Thomas had chosen this thing that looked like a giant redwood. It was immense! The props team had put this platform in there for me, but I had to be up there on my own. A rope ladder was dangling down from this platform and I must have looked like a broken puppet trying to get up there. Several of the cameramen thought I was playing up to the cameras, but I was going through all stages of terror. To top the whole thing off, as soon as the shot had been rehearsed, Gerald called a tea break and left me up there, saying there wasn't time for me to get down and then

back up again!'

Carry On Cowboy was the most violent *Carry On* to date, but Rothwell defended the shootings by explaining that the audience were sophisticated enough not to be fooled. 'You can't pull the wool over their eyes, you can't cheat them and have someone getting up after they'd been shot, saying, "Oh dear, I've been shot." A bullet would kill and you can't hide that fact. Ask any child who plays Cowboys and Indians and he'll tell you that once you get hit by an Indian's arrow or a Cowboy's bullet, that's it, you're dead. Just because we're making a *Carry On* film doesn't mean we can't bring a certain degree of reality to it.'

With *Cowboy* complete, Rothwell turned his attentions to the gothic horror genre. His inspiration came from the Hammer Horror films which had first made an impact on both sides of the Atlantic in 1957 with *The Curse of Frankenstein* and *Dracula*. Apart from making stars out of Christopher Lee and Peter Cushing, the films had revived the horror genre which cinema audiences loved, and so *Carry On Screaming* was born.

Sid James was unavailable for the filming date of February 1966, so Rogers and Thomas looked for another familiar face who was popular at the time. The choice they made came from the world of the sitcom. Harry H. Corbett from *Steptoe and Son* was soon contracted to them, working alongside Peter Butterworth, who, like Bresslaw, had joined the team with *Cowboy*. Location shooting this time took place in the woods near Windsor Castle and Fulmer, while interior shots took place within the studio confines of Pinewood.

Screaming was Corbett's only venture into

Bernard Bresslaw in drag yet again for
Carry On Doctor

Screaming **was Harry H. Corbett's (left) only** ***Carry On***

the world of *Carry On* and in one interview he gave, he explained why he had enjoyed the experience so much: 'It was like a send-up of Sherlock Holmes. I was given a deer-stalker and a pipe, so I played up to it. Detective Sergeant Bung was a fool who didn't realise he was one and the whole thing was a pleasure to be involved in.'

Originally Hawtrey was not to appear in this film, but when word leaked out to the press, Thomas had to revise the casting. Hawtrey was immensely popular among cinema-going audiences and it was felt that his absence could have resulted in diminished box-office returns, so he was quickly slipped into the film, playing the character of Dan Dan, his briefest appearance ever in the series.

Williams vividly remembered the final scene of *Screaming*, which required his villainous character, Doctor Watt, to be dragged to his death in a vat of boiling hot wax by the reanimated mummy, Rubbatiti. As he explained in an interview given at the time of the film's release: 'This great trough was full of the most appalling liquid which smelled like something unmentionable and tasted even worse. I had to actually go under this substance and then leap out and cry "Frying tonight!" in one take. The wretched stuff was so foul that we had to do the scene in one take because it seriously damaged the fabric of my clothing. I went over to Gerald Thomas and said, "Damn the costume, what about me?", and with a straight face he looked at me and replied, "Well, we'll just have to wait and find out, won't we, Kenneth?".'

Carry On Screaming was the last in the series that Rogers and Thomas made for Anglo-amalgamated. Their association with that company ended after the completion of twelve highly successful films which saw the phrase 'Carry On' change from being just another film title to a household word.

**Sid James in glamorous
disguise for *Don't Lose Your Head***

Chapter 4
All Change

'It's an enigma. That's what it is, Matron, an enigma!
'I'm not having another one of those!'
Kenneth Williams and Sid James, *Carry On Doctor* (1967)

In 1967 Rogers struck a new deal with the Rank Film Organisation, which effectively changed both his financial backers and his distribution company. By now the *Carry On* franchise was extremely lucrative so Rank were canny to take the series on, but their participation in the productions came with a catch. Rank were business rivals with Anglo-Amalgamated who were not happy about their biggest competitors using the 'Carry On' title prefix. Rank did not want to fall into a protracted and expensive legal dispute with Anglo-Amalgamated.

Keen to continue with the historical themes, Rothwell focused his attention on the story of the French Revolution, which, like Cleo, was another tried and trusted theme for major Hollywood film treatments in the past. The title that this new film would have - which was a *Carry On* in all but name - was *Don't Lose Your Head*. Rothwell saw it as a rollicking adventure and wrote the character of Sir Rodney Ffing with Sid James in mind. 'This is Sid James as Errol Flynn, if you like,' he said prior to the film's release. 'It's like one of those swashbuckling romps that were made throughout the 1930s and 1940s, but instead of Flynn there's Sid, and instead of Basil Rathbone there's Kenneth Williams. The only real difference is that this is deliberately funny whereas the originals were never directly humorous. And it's probably the only time you'll ever get to see Sid James in a dress!'

James was far from happy about having to wear a skirt and wig on any occasion, let alone in front of the *Carry On* crew, as he guessed, quite rightly, that the mickey-taking would be unrelenting. Kenneth Williams proposed marriage to him and several of the crew members spent their spare moments trying to chat him up, commenting on his flowing blonde locks and the beautiful texture of his skin. This apparently got to be too much for James, and he was frequently seen swearing and shouting at his tormentors before hoisting up his skirts and heading off towards his dressing room, where he would smoke a pipe, firmly clenched in his teeth.

In order to give the film a polished look and recreate the streets and chateaux of nineteenth century France, extensive location filming was carried out in September 1966, with Waddesdon Manor being used for a week and Clandon Park and Cliveden also being roped in for variety. The budgets were now heading towards the £200,000 mark, but even so, there was no worry on the part of the financing company because the films would make that money back within a couple of weeks of general release.

Don't Lose Your Head saw one of the few occasions when the cast were allowed to come up with an ad-lib that would end up on screen. As far as Thomas was concerned, the scripts were unbreakable and what was on the page was filmed, come what may. In a strange twist of fate it was actually the ad-lib fearing Sid James who came up with the gag. During the sequence when Charles Hawtrey's Duc de Pommefrit is on the executioner's block, James suddenly suggested that someone bring Hawtrey a note and he would chuck it in the basket in front of the block, saying he would read it later.

James would show a remarkable deft hand

***Don't Lose Your Head* included a double wedding and a deadly duel**

at swordsmanship in this film, partnering the athletic Jim Dale for the main fight sequences. In another rare interview to the press on the subject of film-making, James spoke about his faith in and admiration of the fight coordinators: 'You have the most skilled technicians around you at all times, for their job is to ensure you look as good and convincing as you can on screen. They make the ridiculous seem utterly convincing, taking someone like me and turning them into a master swordsman. Take it from me, that takes some doing! They may rib you a little every so often in the process, but at the end of the day their job is exactly the same as yours. You're there to entertain an audience because it's them who make sure you get another job after that, by paying to see you in the first place.'

As work on *Don't Lose Your Head* came to an end, plans were being laid down to try and broaden the appeal of the

films in America, as they had never really matched the success of *Carry On Nurse*. The immediate solution was to import a familiar face from the US comedy circuit, and several tentative approaches were made to various actors before Phil Silvers was settled upon as the ideal man for the job. He had long been a star on stage, and his reputation as a comedy legend was guaranteed by his television series in the 1950s, Sergeant Bilko. Rothwell's script for the next project was therefore a feature-length ambitious Bilko story of Bilko and the French Foreign Legion in the desert.

Like *Don't Lose Your Head*, *Follow That Camel* did not have the *Carry On* tag attached to it, and once again, a cheap alternative to the desert that the storyline called for had to be found. Eventually, three weeks were spent in Camber Sands in Sussex. The only thing that Thomas couldn't fake was the camel. He had to find a real one. In typical *Carry On* tradition he didn't even manage to hire a normal one. Sheena came from Chessington Zoo and the problem was that as soon as she arrived at Camber Sands, the sight of all that open space utterly unsettled her - she was afraid of the sand! She clambered back into her transportation unit and refused to come out. The keeper tried to coax her out but she couldn't bear to put her feet on the shifting sand. A solution was eventually found by laying down boards for her to walk on out of shot. Through the camera lens it looked as if she was at one with her surroundings.

Another disaster involving sand happened

Kenneth Williams with Sheena the camel - Williams is the one in the hat

when Bernard Bresslaw, who had been cast as Sheikh Abdul Abulbul, had to complete a relatively simple sequence in which he leads a band of sword-wielding Arabs on a charge towards the fort.

'Gerald Thomas gave simple instructions along the lines of "Make plenty of noise and scream and shout, wave your swords and go past the camera as quickly as you can",' he recalled. 'Well, I was in the front, and a gang of extras were crowded in behind me, working themselves up for the death charge. As soon as the cameras began to roll and and Gerald shouted "Action!" , my feet became tangled up in my robes and I fell flat on my face. Because the extras were a bit like sheep and just kept going because no one had told them to stop, dozens of feet trampled over me and buried me in the sand.'

Bresslaw was also the subject of some totally unwarranted servile behaviour by a car park attendant near the location shoot, who thought the actor was a visiting VIP. In an interview Bresslaw gave, he remembered the man well. 'I was treated like royalty by this fella. He was bowing and scraping the ground, asking me how I liked this country and was I bothered by the cold weather. It was hysterical and I played up to it for a while. I would arrive every day at this car park in this sleek Rolls-Royce, in full Arab costume and make-up, so I could see why he thought I was a visiting dignitary. But situations like this are so rare and wonderful it's impossible to resist not playing up to them.'

In *Follow That Camel* it was Silvers, naturally enough, who received top billing, but he suffered at the hands of Kenneth

Carry On Laughing

Williams who was unimpressed that the American required cue cards as soon as he arrived on set in case he forgot his lines. This was the way things were done on American television and it was a method that Silvers was used to, but Williams considered cue cards to be the height of unprofessionalism. Silvers also drove Williams up the wall with his barrage of Hollywood anecdotes, ranging from his work with Frank Sinatra to meeting with the Pope. In fact, Rogers had to eventually reprimand Williams for his caustic tongue. Williams recalled in 1982: 'Peter gave me a gentle

Joan Sims as Madame Zigzag, paramour of the much decorated Sergeant Knocker

ticking off. I was being a bit naughty and outrageous, and having the propmen wave damn great sheets of paper around was most off-putting. It

also meant Silvers never looked into your eyes as he was too busy trying to see what his lines were.'

On completion of these two films Rank came to an agreement with Anglo-Amalgamated that the 'Carry On' prefix should be reinstated on all future films. The first of these went back to the world of bedpans and matrons, and was christened

Doctor Tinkle falls foul of Nurse May in
Carry On Doctor

Carry On Doctor. In 1969, two years after
work had been finished on *Don't Lose Your
Head* and *Follow That Camel*, the title
sequences for both films were reshot to bring
them into the official *Carry On* series. All
future prints that were made of those movies
bore the 'Carry On' prefix and all future
catalogue references carried the new full
titles as well.

Sid James, absent from *Carry On ... Follow
That Camel* due to a heart condition,
returned to the *Carry On* fold with *Doctor* as
bed-bound Charlie Roper. In this Rogers

and Thomas were being considerate; they
didn't want James to tire himself out but
they wanted him in the film nonetheless as
the audiences loved him. It was only during
the last six weeks of filming, when the
patients rebel against Matron and Doctor
Tinkle, that James was allowed to get up on
his feet and start work properly again.

With *Carry On Nurse* still ranking as one of
the most popular films made by Rogers and
Thomas, it was logical to try and recapture
that film's magic a second time. Work began
on *Carry On Doctor* midway through
September 1967, with Rothwell aiming for
the jugular of the medical profession in his
script, which he later admitted was one of

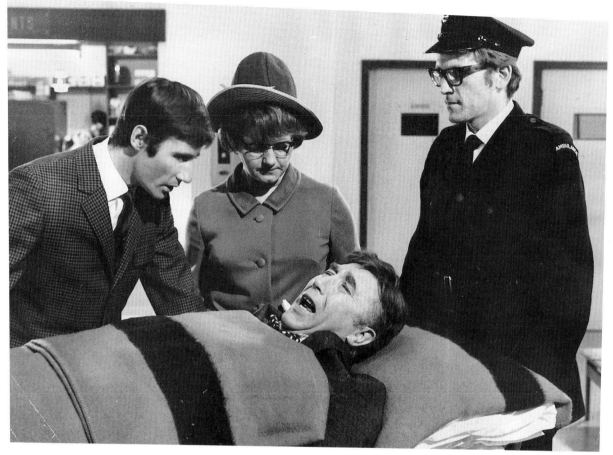

Frankie Howerd guest starred in *Carry On Doctor* as Francis Bigger

his favourites to write: 'I'm afraid I've never been the greatest fan of the National Health Service, or the way in which hospitals operate, so I just couldn't resist putting in that whole scene where Frankie Howerd is trying to get some sleep and all manner of chaos is breaking out around him, with tea trolleys arriving in the middle of the night and the cleaners making a dreadful noise. Friends always tell me after they've seen the film that their experience of hospitals was just like that, which makes that scene even more funny. Who says the *Carry Ons* have no comment to make about society? I have to say that when writing the films, I get my own back on society!'

Frankie Howerd's career was going through a renaissance in the mid to late 1960s. He languished at the end of the 1950s but was brought back into the limelight as an act in Peter Cook's infamous club, The Establishment, which led to an appearance on the satirical show on the BBC, *That Was The Week That Was*. His performance on that show went down so well that he was soon back in demand on other television programmes and theatres throughout the country, and by 1967 he was a big enough star to warrant top billing in a *Carry On* film.

Although Howerd appeared only twice in the *Carry On* films (*Carry On Up The Jungle* was his second outing) he was generally regarded as being a natural member of the *Carry On* team, a fact that continued to haunt him for many years, as he explained in an interview in 1987.

'When I go on holiday I really like to go far, so there's been the odd trip to the Far East and the West Indies, but wherever it is, people seem to recognise me from those two *Carry On*s. I don't know what on earth all those foreigners are saying to me, but when the words 'Carry On' crop up, I think I can guess. There was one occasion, when I was out in the middle of nowhere in Borneo, in a village full of mud huts, one slightly larger shack acted as a local cinema. And guess what was showing? A bloody *Carry On* film! And to make it even worse, it was *Carry On Up The Jungle*!'

At the end of *Carry On Doctor* the patients rebel, as they did in *Carry On Nurse*, and both Hattie Jacques' Matron and Kenneth Williams' Dr Tinkle are punished for the torture they had inflicted upon the long-suffering patients. In one sequence, Williams is seen being dumped into a bath tub full of ice cubes, which were supposed to be lumps of plastic cut into ice cube shapes. Bernard Bresslaw explained during the promotional interviews given at the time of the film's release that that wasn't actually the case: 'There was a certain amount of revenge involved in that bit, because Kenneth used to drive people around the twist with all his practical jokes and rude

The Third Foot And Mouth encounter the rampaging Burpas

For the eagle-eyed viewer there's evidence of an in-joke between Peter Rogers and his wife to be spotted. It can be found in every scene where the doors of the hospital lifts are on show. While Rogers had been ploughing through countless *Carry On* films, his wife, Betty Box, was still producing the *Doctor* films, with Ralph Thomas directing. Rogers had already cleared the fact that his team were using the

remarks. The chance to use real ice was just too much for people to be able to resist. When all the ice was poured on top of him the amazing thing was that he just kept on going, right though until Gerald called "cut!". After that, the air was as blue as Kenneth was!'

all of Box's *Doctor* films, and so in *Carry On Doctor* a bizarre link was formed by having his picture hung in their hospital by the lift doors!

Doctor was an immediate success and by mutual agreement Rogers and Thomas decided to return to another old theme for the next film. They chose the army. Rothwell was keen to bring a Bulldog Drummond-esque story to the screen, with a *Carry On* treatment of the long-passed *Boys' Own* style of story telling that had been so popular in the 1920s and 1930s. Hence *Carry On Up the Khyber* was drafted - with just a little bit of influence from the popular film *Zulu* which had recently been released.

Naturally, there was no way that the budget for the film would stretch to filming in India, so as usual, an alternative location had to be found. Kenneth Williams recalled the story: 'They went to Snowdon! I mean, what kind of substitute for the gracious beauty of India is that? Charlie Hawtrey didn't enjoy a single minute of it, said the

Charles Hawtrey (left) paints the famous 'thin red line' and Terry Scott conducts a kit inspection (above)

word 'Doctor' in their rival series with his wife, by giving her a percentage of the royalties made on *Carry On Doctor*, and as an affectionate nod of appreciation, one of the artists at Pinewood was commissioned to produce an oil painting of James Robertson-Justice. Robertson-Justice had played Sir Lancelot Spratt, the head of the hospital in wind was far too icy and it kept on lifting the kilt up around his head. It ended up with the costume team sewing lead weights into the lining, just to keep his rear hidden from view. Peter Rogers actually has this amazing story about being called away from the set of the film because he had to attend some important function where Princess Margaret as the guest of honour. She was introduced to him, and obviously being a woman of refined taste knew all about the *Carry On* films. She asked Peter where Gerald Thomas was, and I don't know how he managed to keep a straight face, but he looked at her and replied, "Up Snowdon, Ma'am.'"

Peter Butterworth became the target of a mass practical joke which the entire cast and crew pulled on him during the filming of what is perhaps the most famous *Carry On* scene of all. At the climax of *Khyber* the home of Sir Sidney Ruff-Diamond is under siege, with the massed forces of the Khasi of Kalabar trying to take over the British army's base. Whilst all this is going on outside, Sir Sidney and his guests are trying to enjoy their evening meal as the room literally falls in around their ears.

This scene took over one and a half days to film. By the morning of the second day, the

Terry Scott played Sergeant Major McNutt

food on the table was going off and the cast were covered with bits of plaster and dust, so were far from being happy. Butterworth explained what happened at the scene's

climax, in an interview he gave in 1975.

'The roof was meant to cave in and bury everyone under all of this rubbish and my character was supposed to dive under the table. Once there I couldn't see a thing due to all the dust in the air. The only thing that I could hear was Gerald Thomas's voice calling out, telling Sid and the others to keep going as the cameras were still rolling. I just stayed under the table and after a few minutes I realised that the whole studio was silent, but I didn't move in case I spoiled the shot. After about another five minutes I became certain that something had gone wrong, and poked my nose out from underneath the table. The whole place was empty... Gerald had kept calling out while everyone left for lunch, knowing full well that I would stay under the table. When I got to the canteen, Gerald looked me up and down and with an evil glint in his eye, he said, "What kept you?"'

Carry On Up the Khyber is cited by many of the regular cast and crew as being their favourite of the entire series, both to work on and as the completed film. A couple of years later, on the set of *Carry On Henry*, Sid

James, who rarely passed any form of critical comment on his work to the press, admitted that *Khyber* was a personal favourite, commenting: 'Everything looks just right. When money is as tight as it is on these films, you're sometimes lucky if the finished product is convincing. *Carry On Up the Khyber* just rings true and to this day I'm not sure how we did it.'

Terry Scott, who had returned to the series after appearing last in *Carry On Sergeant*, also spoke about the film in a 1984 interview. 'I played a character called Sergeant-Major McNutt in *Carry On Up the Khyber*.

It was a wonderful opportunity to do one of those really abrasive, tight-arsed Colonel Blimp types, and we really all had a lot of fun in the process. The kilt took a bit of getting used to. I remember Peter Butterworth turning to me after a take where I'd bawled out Charles Hawtrey, and said, "Did you pay them to give you this part, or are you doing it for free?" I think it must have been so obvious that I was thoroughly enjoying myself!'

Apart from being one of the most financially successful of all the

The Khasi of Kalabar

*Carry On*s at the box-office, the film can also lay claim to being one of the most authentic visually, due to the fact that after seeing the film, a former army officer got in contact with Peter Rogers to tell him how delighted he had been to see the Khyber Pass again as he'd actually served out there during his young days. Bernard Bresslaw related a similar incident: 'It was one of those occasions when you haven't got the heart to tell people the truth. I went into an Indian restaurant in Newcastle, and the owner greeted me as if I were a long-lost relative. He'd seen *Carry On Up the Khyber* and was delighted to see his home country on the big screen. He immediately asked me if I'd enjoyed my stay in India while we were making the film, and I really didn't know what to say!'

Holidays came under the *Carry On* spotlight once again, following on from *Cruising*, and the second film of the year began filming in early October with the cast bravely pretending that *Carry On Camping* was actually set in the height of summer when in fact they were subjected to an unending stream of drizzle and rain. Being late autumn, there were barely any leaves left on the trees in the orchard in Pinewood's backlot which served as the film's camp site, and the persistent rain had turned the grass into a sea of mud.

Prop men, armed with spray guns filled with bright green paint, were duly

All the regulars went camping in the fifteenth *Carry On*

summoned to spray the ground of the
orchard, while the remaining leaves were
camouflaged with dark green paint.
Unfortunately, although the ground now
looked a convincing green, it didn't stop the
cast from sinking in the mud just as soon as
they stepped into the orchard. Bernard
Bresslaw explained how they managed to
solve that problem.

'The prop men went off and got these huge
sections of board and flat metal grilles,
which were laid out on the ground in a

Going, going . . .

careful route around the orchard. This
meant we could stride along and look as
though the grass was firm and solid. It was
like wandering into a swamp of quicksand if
you so much as strayed off that path. The
extras were the ones who really suffered,
because while we were on the boards and
the cameras were rolling, they were doing
what extras do in the background, literally

sinking to their knees in green mud! People were going through hell and they had to be pulled out at the end of the take, and all the time they had to look as though they were enjoying themselves!'

The infamous exercise scene was shot on a day where the outside temperature was heading towards zero and the bulk of the female cast were standing around in their bikinis. Williams' Doctor Soper was required to stand before his class of girls and instruct them in some keep fit movements. As Barbara Windsor's character throws out her arms, her bikini top snaps and hits Doctor Soper in the face. At least, that's how Rothwell had planned the sequence, but Kenneth Williams recalled what really happened.

'Barbara had to have this prop man loop a piece of fishing line through her bra, so that he could stand out of shot with a fishing rod, halfway up a ladder, and yank it off on cue. You've never seen such a performance in your life! This man thought he was going to kill her if he wasn't careful and poor Barbara thought that she'd be flashing her boobs on screen for all to see, so she came up with this plan to clasp her hands over herself as soon as her top came away. Well, for the first few seconds it seemed

to have worked, but then Hattie pulled her arm too hard because she was meant to drag her away, and Barbara lost her grip on her left asset ... I suppose you could say that she ended up half-flashing!'

During filming Windsor made her feelings known to Williams on the working conditions on set. Without either of them realising it, her entire tirade of invective against Rogers and Thomas was recorded on tape, because Williams' throat microphone had been left switched on. When the rushes for that particular day were screened, her words were heard across the speakers in the screening room for all to hear. Windsor genuinely thought that Rogers would sack her as a consequence, but in fact he had already known about the tape. It was him and Thomas who organised the tape to be played at the screening, as their way of getting back at her!

Windsor's words about never wanting to work for the two of them again came back time and time again to haunt her. Whenever she arrived on set to begin work on any new *Carry On*, she was always greeted by the director and the producer in the same way. 'Come back to be treated

. . . gone!

like muck again, eh, Barbara?' It soon became a running joke between the three of them.

Bernard Bresslaw remembered another incident from *Carry On Camping*, involving Charles Hawtrey and a particular kind of food. 'Charles really suffered for his art in that film. There's a scene where Terry Scott pours a tin of baked beans all over him. Charles was sitting there in his vest and underpants while Gerald was pouring the stuff all over him with a ladle for the close-up shots. Charles really hated baked beans and that made it all the worse for him. I can clearly remember him stiffly walking back into his dressing room, a bright shade of orange, asking if I thought it was too late for him to change his career.'

The decision was quickly made to make the next *Carry On* another medical one, because they were so popular. It was Rothwell who came up with the logical title of *Carry On Again Doctor*. Many of the regulars found themselves playing the same kind of role they had had in *Carry On Doctor*, only their names were slightly different. Jim Dale was once again the accident-prone young doctor, Williams the nostril-flaring head surgeon, and as ever, Jacques was the matron. Rothwell remembers: 'Kenneth and Hattie had a marvellous ability to spark off each other. They knew exactly how each other's mechanics operated because they'd

Dr Nookey, Dr Carver and Dr Stoppidge (disguised as Lady Puddleton)

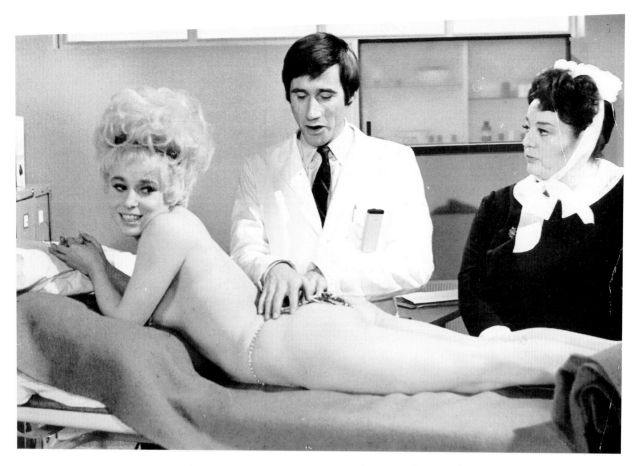

**Goldie Locks is examined
by Dr Nookey**

worked together so often and for so long. She was practically the only person on set who could shut him up with a Paddington Bear-like stare when he was getting a bit carried away. Sometimes there would be an argument between him and some unsuspecting victim, and Hattie would move in to break it up. I can see what she meant when she said Kenneth was like her naughty little brother.'

Carry On Again Doctor was the last time Jim Dale would appear in the series until the one-off revival in 1992, Carry On Columbus. Dale had effectively become the romantic lead in the films and proved to be immensely popular with the other members of the team. His decision to move on to more challenging and classical roles caused slight upset among some of the other regulars. Bresslaw

explained why this was so: 'Jim was part of our family; you could always rely on the fact that he would be there along with Charlie, Sid and Kenneth. I missed out on Carry On Again Doctor and from what I understand, they wanted him for the Tarzan role in Carry On Up the Jungle, but Jim was heading towards the National Theatre and he turned it down. There were one or two comments about him thinking we weren't good enough for him anymore, but I'm sure that wasn't the case.'

Dale had always made a point of doing his own stuntwork whenever he was allowed to: he had really dived off the stagecoach in Carry On Cowboy and he proved to be a genuinely competent swordsman in *Carry On ... Don't Lose Your Head.* In *Carry On Again Doctor* he performed what probably was his most hair-raising feat of all, riding down a stairway on a gurney. Dale admitted at the time that 'there are times when you can't fool the audience because it becomes all too clear that a stuntman has taken your place. I don't want to be guilty of that when I can avoid it. The advantage is that I've been trained in dance techniques, and I can fall and jump so that I don't end up in a wheelchair in the process. The trick is to make it look as though it's more impossible than it actually is. There was one moment in *Carry On ... Follow That Camel* where I had to fall down the neck of a camel and land on the most easily hurt of all places. The completed effect looked dreadfully painful when in fact it was all down to the way you pulled off the trick. In *Carry On Again Doctor* I'm on the gurney, and it looks hair-raising, but if you put your faith in what the stuntmen tell you to do, you come out in one piece.' In fact, in this particular stunt, Dale injured his arm.

In *Carry On Again Doctor* once again Charles Hawtrey donned drag, and Kenneth Williams had a tale to tell about that: 'Charlie had several vicious boils on his nether regions, so he was quite happy about having to wear a dress because it hung quite loosely around the affected area. Well, there was a point where we had a few minutes to kill between set-ups and he kept disappearing whenever this happened into his dressing room, always making it back before Gerald called "action" again. On one occasion he was late back, so a poor girl was sent to find him. There was this almighty

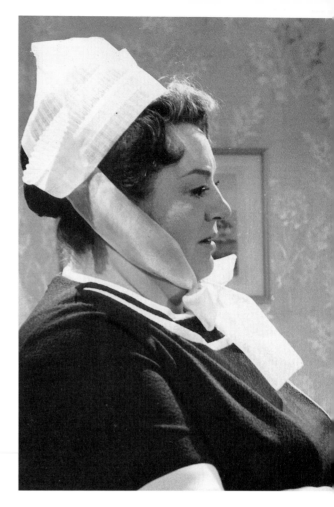

Gladstone Screwer proposes a blood marriage to Matron

scream from the corridor so Sid and I went running to see what had happened. She'd walked into his dressing room and had been confronted by Charlie's buttocks in mid-air, because he'd hoisted his skirt over his head and was smearing ointment onto his sore spot. The poor woman had nearly died of shock!'

Sid James's role in *Carry On Again Doctor* was fairly secondary, with his character making a late appearance in the film, way beyond its halfway point. Williams thought this was a mistake, and even though he had had his differences with James over the

adventure story that Rothwell had been working on since *Carry On Doctor*, went into production next. *Carry On Up The Jungle* started filming in 1969. It took a dig at all the Tarzan films of the 1930s and 1940s; Rothwell was proud of the fact he could take the mickey out of these classics so blatantly.

'If it was an old Tarzan film, you'd have Lex Barker on a vine swinging though the trees, landing on the ground, diving into the water and wrestling with a crocodile before taking on a rampaging gorilla. Once we'd added a touch of *Carry On* sauce, you'd have Tarzan swinging through the trees, accidentally tearing his loincloth as he does so, before landing butt first in a holly bush and rolling into a river screaming in pain, where he's chased by a crocodile straight into the arms of a randy gorilla who's taken quite a shine to him. That's the kind of route we'd take when corrupting an old classic. You had to show no mercy with a *Carry On* script because the first rule of writing them was that nothing should remain sacred.

Kenneth Williams turned down the part of Tonka, which was offered to Charles Hawtrey instead. Terry Scott was the other replacement in the plans which Thomas had for the original casting, as Dale no longer wished to take part. Scott, therefore, became Jungle Boy, and suffered a major humiliating experience practically as soon as he donned his loincloth for the role.

'Jungle Boy was somewhat lacking in the brain department. In the first scene between him and Sid James's character I was told by Gerald to come charging out of the undergrowth, grunting and growling and waving my arms around, that sort of thing. So that's what I did. I remember noticing

years, he also acknowledged that it was his presence which was one of the key elements behind the success of the films. 'When people settle down to watch a *Carry On* film, and I make this observation based on years of correspondence with various people who have written to me, they expect to see all the characters they've grown accustomed to seeing, and they want to see them quickly. Whether it's Sid, Hattie, Charlie or myself, if we don't appear, the viewer is left wanting. *Carry On Again Doctor* left out Sid for nearly an hour and his sudden arrival was jarring. I always felt that was a mistake.'

Nevertheless, *Carry On Again Doctor* was a success, and the second *Boys' Own*

Jungle Boy with jungle loin cloth thankfully covering his jungle bits

the cameraman was shaking the camera with laughing so much; even Gerald had to turn away from me to stifle his laughter. I thought, "You're doing well here, son, keep it going!" so I became more and more wild until Sid lost it completely and pointed to my loincloth. It was then I'd realised why there was so much laughter. My arms were not the only things that were being waved about. Damn loincloths!'

Bernard Bresslaw yet again donned dark make-up to play a native, Upsidasi, the tribe's leader. In an effort to avoid making up gibberish when it came to speaking to his men in their native tongue, as the script dictated, Bresslaw went out of his way to get it right.

'My bearers were played by Africans so I really wanted to try and learn some phrases that were authentic. I asked my brother Stan to help because he knew how to speak Ndebele, which is a language native to Zimbabwe. This wasn't easy by any stretch of the imagination but I cracked it in the end and went onto the set on the first day full of pride and confidence.

that the rest of the cast were having a huge problem in trying to keep a straight face and

I just couldn't wait to get to the scene where we had to emerge out of the jungle and I had to tell them what to do.

'Right on cue I rattled off a whole stream of Ndebelese, which went something along the lines of, "Put the boxes down as we must set up camp for our masters." The bearers looked at me blankly and then Gerald told me that they weren't Africans at all, but West Indians! However, it paid off in the end because a few years later I was stopped by the owner of a shoe shop in Bournemouth who asked me where I'd learnt to speak Ndebelese so fluently! He was very impressed as he'd grown up in Zimbabwe!'

Sid James and Joan Sims facing the terrors of the jungle

Sid James was renowned for enjoying an occasional flutter on the horses and playing cards. In fact he'd always set up a card table on whatever film he was working on and *Carry On Up the Jungle* proved to be no exception. However, on this occasion the only players he could muster were Terry Scott and Reuben Martin, the actor who played the gorilla. So, the unwary visitor to the set of the film would have seen James in a corner playing poker between takes with a primitive man and an ape! Terry Scott recalled: 'Sid's rules of poker were unique; there was always the odd twist and turn here and there which always brought the hand down in his favour. Well, the guy in the gorilla suit was no fool and he gave as good as he got. In the wilds of Africa the Great White Hunter would have shot the animal dead. In Pinewood, they stood up shouting at each other until the director would wade in and break them up! You never knew what you were going to get when you worked with Gerald and Peter!'

Audiences adored whatever the *Carry On* team chose to serve up to them during the mid to late 1960s, because *Carry On Up the Jungle* proved to be another immense success, but as a new decade began, a far more blatantly suggestive film was planned. Rothwell justified this by saying he was keen to keep the series up to date with trends in society. The late 1960s were promiscuous, with the preaching of free love and the hippy

Horrified by a discovery in the jungle (above) and horrified to discover the ape's got no cash (left)

movement, and the younger generation were becoming far more aware sexually than they ever were in my day. Advertising campaigns started using sex as a selling aid, and it was at about that time that the newspaper page three girls began to appear. *Carry On Loving* was entirely geared towards the way society was heading. I believe we hit the mood of the times with that one, and I believe we got it right.'

Carry On Loving saw the return of Kenneth Williams to the fold, and at the film's press launch he said he was glad to be back. 'Well, yes, I have been away, and to use a terrible cliche, absence does make the heart grow fonder! Gerald and Peter are like extended family, because every time they bring their flock together, after you've been away, they make you feel extraordinarily welcome to be back. People were just so nice to me, saying how much they'd missed me on the last film, although if you'd told me that I'd still be making *Carry On* films today when we started in 1958, I'd have been of a mind to recommend that you have yourself committed! Nobody knew, and who could

together congregating at a banquet, where a vast food fight breaks out. Even Williams got a pie in his face, as he remembered well: 'The whole scene revolved around me getting a cream pie in the face, and of course, everybody wanted to have a go at this!

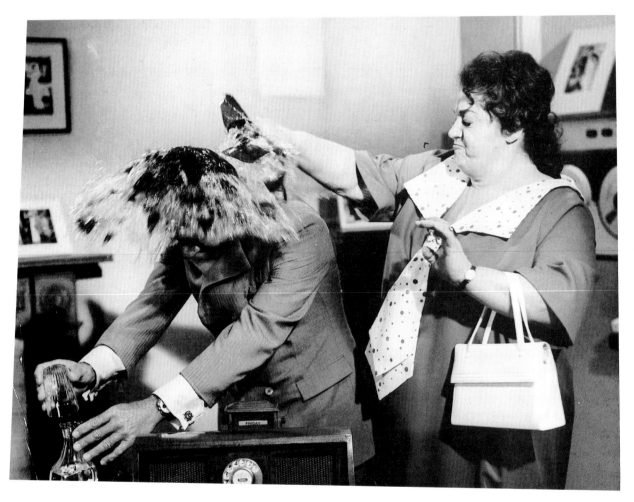

honestly have known that they would be going for so long.'

Carry On Loving was the first time that the team used the old comedy failsafe of a pie fight at the end of the film, with all the not-so-happy couples that Sid James and Hattie Jacques' Wedded Bliss Agency had brought

In *Carry On Loving*, Sid James cops it from Hattie Jacques . . .

Gerald, being Gerald, pushed his way to the front of the queue and called out "Action!", threw the pie and missed me completely. Well, I'd asked for someone cross-eyed in the first place to do it, and now I knew I'd certainly got one! He tried again and missed me by miles, so of course the taunting started and I revelled in every glorious minute of it. I was Williams the conqueror, Williams the triumphant, Williams the

routine; "And it's a glorious day here at Pinewood, with not a soul in sight capable of cracking the shell of the mighty Williams", for of course Julian missed me by a mile as well. It was a distance of no more than a few feet and they all floundered.'

victorious, impervious to all pies! Gerald tried yet again, and hit the wall. The man's aim was as accurate as a bent rifle and I was certain that he'd never get me.

'Julian Holloway was a crack bowler so in the end Gerald wheeled him in and I duly went into my Brian Johnson at the Oval

. . . while Kenneth Williams and Patsy Rowlands cop it in the great food fight

At the press conference it was Bresslaw who took up this particular Williams story. 'Julian Holloway couldn't hit him and by now Kenneth was ranting and raving, being unmerciful with that acid tongue he had,' he recalled. 'I threw one, and it just seemed to glide through the air in slow motion and fall behind him, and he spat out, "For goodness sake, Bernard, you could just reach across and get me with that one!" This must have gone on for over half an hour, and the place was in uproar. I think it was Lauri (Lupino) Lane who got him in the end, straight in his mouth. As far as I remember, Gerald called for a lunch break as soon as he'd got the shot, because we were all too exhausted to do any more.'

Carry On Loving was another big hit, proving Rothwell's theory about moving with the times to be correct. It was at this time that he began to scout around for a new subject. While *Loving* was being filmed, a situation similar to the one surrounding *Cleopatra* was arising, with another major movie gaining a huge amount of daily press attention. It starred Elizabeth Taylor's then-husband Richard Burton in a historical epic about Henry VIII

Alexandra Dane and Ronnie Brody in *Carry On Loving*

Henry VIII pondering his next affair of state

called *Anne of a Thousand Days*. With all that media attention, the long deceased monarch quickly became the ideal target for the *Carry On* treatment.

The first thing that had to be done was to secure permission to film various scenes around a castle of regal proportions, and with a remarkable piece of luck, the Royal Household gave permission for the *Carry On* unit to film on the Long Walk which leads up to Windsor Castle. The rest of the location shooting took place in Windsor Great Park and Pinewood Studios. The film had been called *Carry On Henry* and Sid James had the starring role. As usual, he only gave a brief interview with the press about his thoughts on the film, but he was full of

Scott and Williams as Wolsey and Cromwell

praise for Thomas and Peters: 'These *Carry On* films never have the uphill struggle that you feel others have to face with their movies. Gerald Thomas and Peter Rogers have an almost mechanical system of making these films, and no one can fault them for doing them wrong. Do you think we'd all be here right now, making the 21st *Carry On* film, if they had?'

James also praised the high quality of the film's costumes, which added to the already authentic look that the sets were achieving. After laughing, he explained: 'I'm wearing Richard Burton's hand-me-downs! I can still smell his aftershave on the collar. When we did *Carry On Cleo*, Peter salvaged lots of stuff from the original *Cleopatra* and I think he's done the same here. I think the *Carry On* motto must be "Beg, Borrow and Film"!'

Having been stretched on the rack, Sir Roger signs his confession

Carry On Henry actually proved quite costly to make, with the budget nudging the £225,000 mark. Williams once flippantly observed that he could tell when things cost more than usual as there were more moths flying out of Peter Rogers' wallet.

Having missed out on several of the 1960s *Carry On*s, Kenneth Connor had returned as a series regular in *Up the Jungle* and made a brief appearance in *Henry* as Sir Hampton of Wick. One of the scenes he witnessed involved Kenneth Williams putting Charles Hawtrey on the rack in his torture chamber in order to force a confession out of him. Connor recalled the incident: 'Hawtrey is seen getting longer and longer every time Williams cranked the rack. Charles was a quiet man but was quite capable of the odd remark that was equal to anything Kenneth could say. When the scene was over he turned to the props man and asked, "Does this thing really stretch human limbs?" The technician looked a bit nonplussed and said,

"Well, I suppose it does," and Charles looked him up and down and said, "Come into my room afterwards because I have a bit of freelance work for you. And bring your smallest rack." Kenneth Williams' jaw nearly hit the floor while Charles just looked as if butter wouldn't have melted in his mouth!'

Although *Carry On Henry* kept up the *Carry On* track record in terms of financial returns at the box-office, the entire climate of the film industry was now beginning to change, and it was becoming increasingly difficult for even the most successful producers to secure full financing for their projects. Peter Rogers had seen this coming and began to take measures as far back as

Still competing to steal the scene even as they're about to lose their heads

in 1969 to ensure that the *Carry On* series would continue, if ever the day came when money for film-making dried out, on an entirely different medium. That medium was television.

A series of one-hour specials were made, which Rothwell scripted. The innuendoes were still present with the titles going as far as the memorable Christmas special, *Carry On Stuffing*. The first of these specials to be produced, *Carry On Christmas*, proved to be the most popular single programme broadcast over the entire Christmas period in 1969. All the regulars were there with the exception of Kenneth Williams, who refused to make the transition into this new medium, having fallen out of love with it during his experiences on *Hancock's Half Hour*. Speaking in 1985

explained his reluctance to take part in the specials: 'When the *Carry On*s moved to television, that was it as far as I was

Charles Hawtrey in Thames Television's 1969 special *Carry On Christmas*

Santa and his little helper

concerned. I just didn't want to know. I stayed with the films, a fact that's clearly there for all to see, but as far as the TV specials went, I just couldn't be bothered and more importantly, I couldn't see the point.'

In the following year Rogers and Thomas offered *Carry On Again Christmas*. Although studio-bound, the target of these programmes was to send up the literary classics that were usually the subject of a high-budget adaptation in the Yuletide period. Specials that were made included Sid James as Scrooge and Long John Silver, with Barbara Windsor playing the Christmas Fairy.

The movies did keep going alongside the Christmas specials, and as 1971 began, the first of the two *Carry Ons* for that year got underway. *Carry On At Your Convenience* tackled the British trade unions, and Rothwell was very clear as to why he had made them his choice of target: 'There was nothing new in the news and on television except strikes, strikes and yet more strikes. Union leaders were becoming celebrities in their own right; I remember seeing one signing autographs for kids as he went into a conference centre, and when I later found out that he was the boss of a toilet factory, apart from having hysterics I started working on a script sending up the whole shop steward business. The temptation was there to call the factory 'S. Hitter and Sons' or 'Dump & Wipe Ltd' but good taste prevailed and we settled for 'W. C. Boggs & Son' instead!'

Bernard Bresslaw had fond memories from this film - he recalled becoming unstuck in a most embarrassing way: 'When asked, actors say they can do anything that's required, like riding a horse, even if they've never been on the animal in their lives. It happened with me and motorbikes. Of course I said I could ride one and I didn't let Peter Rogers know the truth until the morning that we were due to shoot this bit where I come down the street on this monstrous machine, glide to a halt and get off it, looking like I've been doing that sort of thing all my life. When I told Peter the truth, to say his face went pale would be an understatement. He was almost transparent. During the lunch break he got

The W. C. Boggs staff on their annual outing

Jacques and James were married yet again in *At Your Convenience*

the production manager's son to teach me the basics and it got to the point that I could just about manage to drive the bike in a straight line and stop it successfully. That was good enough for Gerald, because he had decided to use a double in all other shots. One shot did, however, require me to park by the kerb and get off the thing. It should have been easy enough but no, the thing stalled, it fell over, the stand wouldn't come down and I got my jacket sleeve caught in the handlebars. It went to about 25 takes before Gerald gave up - the crew was laughing so much we couldn't go on. He told us he'd patch it all together out of what we had managed to do, but in the end he cut the scene all together.'

For the first time, Rogers and Thomas made a *Carry On* flop. By ridiculing the unions, it alienated the audiences who were the series' biggest fans. Normally, production costs on a *Carry On* film were made back after a few weeks of general release. It took close to five years to make back the money spent on *Carry On At Your Convenience*.

Convenience marked the end of the string of hits that Rogers and Thomas had been making. Rothwell had completed the script for the next film, *Carry On Matron*, guaranteeing that the audience that

Jacki Piper played Sid's daughter and married the boss's son Richard O'Callaghan

was lost with the last effort would return in droves to see the world of the bedpan, syringes and stethoscopes, but the writing was on the wall. During the course of the next few years the *Carry On* films would gradually die out.

Kenneth Cope and Terry Scott as Cyril Carter and Dr Prodd

Chapter 5

Bedpans, Big Dick and the French Ambassador's Wife

*'No, I don't believe in free love, and what's more, I think it's
very insulting of you to ask!'*
'Well, you don't believe in paying for it, do you?'
Hattie Jacques and Kenneth Williams, *Carry On Matron* (1971)

'I know it sounds awfully strange, but there have been one or two people who've come up to me in the street, asking me about their aches and pains and I think they should have this done or that done, and it was never a case of calling me Hattie or even Miss Jacques ... it was always "Matron", and that was due entirely to the medical *Carry On* films. A man who stopped me for an autograph once asked me if I could put "Matron" underneath my signature. I think it's what I'll be remembered for, and I have no complaints about that at all.'

Hattie Jacques' reputation among fellow actors, and especially in the *Carry On* team, can only be described as glowing. She was more than popular with all of them and always took the time to talk to anybody who stopped her for her autograph, as the above quote clearly shows. Next to *Carry On Cabby*, *Carry On Matron* was her favourite *Carry On*, as she once explained: 'The Matron in the early films was always a

sharp and austere character who nobody particularly cared for, and one always thought the audiences would cheer when she got her come-uppance. The Matron in *Carry On Matron* was different; this was a woman who cared and was in complete contrast to the earlier one. Because of that new softness I felt she was the more successful of the two.'

Filming on *Carry On Matron* began at Pinewood during the second week of October 1971, and saw the arrival of Jack Douglas as a regular member of the team. It was, however, Terry Scott's last appearance in a *Carry On* film, and it appeared to be one of his favourites, as the actor said at the time. 'I spent some time in hospital a few years ago, and one of the doctors fancied himself as a bit of a matinee idol. He was all over the nurses and for reasons best left to the imagination, they had given him the nickname of Doctor Prod, which I thought was funny. And that's the character I play in *Carry On Matron*!'

The drag acts returned in force for that film, with Kenneth Cope spending a large part of the film in a nurse's uniform and Bernard Bresslaw donning a full maternity gown in the finale. Bresslaw was not the only one to have had great fun in the breaks between shooting that scene. The thing about having to wear a dress when you're a man is that it feels so odd, and on any other film you'd want to get out of it as quickly as possible, but during the *Carry Ons* people seem to have become possessed and Kenneth Cope was particularly guilty of this, flashing his suspenders at the technicians and chasing after them with his skirts in the air. They were all terrified of him and I have to admit, and bow my head

Wrong door, surely?

Kenneth Cope is exposed while Bernard Bresslaw keeps mum

in shame, that even without padding I looked a convincing nine months pregnant.

'One lunchtime, the canteen was packed and Kenneth Williams and I couldn't get a seat anywhere, so he pushed me though shouting, "Make way! Make way! There's an expectant mother here!" because I was still in my frock. Then these riggers got up and gave us their table. Kenneth was very gracious as they left, and then burst out laughing when I told him it had been my performance that had done it. He then pointed out that they must have been exceptionally thick, as there aren't too many expectant mothers who are six foot seven with stubble on their chins!'

Williams had a great deal of trouble

learning all the medical terms and expressions and barely got through the medical *Carry On*s, so Gerald Thomas decided to have a bit of fun at his expense, as Williams explained: 'Tolly [Talbot Rothwell] had come up with an entire scene of complex medical jargon which was infuriating, as one never knows how to pronounce these things. I knew he had done this on Gerald's request. Gerald was merciless but eventually we settled for a halfway decent attempt.'

Carry On Matron was followed in 1972 with *Carry On Abroad*, which saw the last appearance in a *Carry On* film by Charles Hawtrey. In total he had starred in over 23 films, but *Abroad* marked his last appearance due to a dispute with Peter Rogers. Once again, as in *Carry On Cruising*, the dispute was over star billing, only this time Hawtrey was not prepared to compromise and severed his links with the *Carry On* team after the completion of another Christmas special.

Carry On Abroad was one of the last really good *Carry On*s. In it, Bresslaw donned a cassock to play a monk who is holidaying with his fellow brethren at the appalling Spanish holiday resort of Elsbels. One scene required him to chase a girl through the glass of the revolving doors at the hotel. Bresslaw remembered the scene well. 'I just tripped. My feet got tangled up in the cassock and I went straight through the glass and ended up in a heap at the other side. There was a deathly silence and I kept quiet, just in case the cameras were still rolling, but nobody said a word so I looked up and said, "Sorry, Gerald, I just tripped over my own feet." He said, "You idiot! You spoke to me! I was going to use that take in the finished film!" Then, with a glint in his eye he always had at moments like that, he said, "Let's go for a retake. You'll have to go it again, Bernard, and I mean through the glass." There was a second's pause when I thought he really meant it!'

Mrs Tuttle (Amelia Bayntum) fusses over her son in *Carry On Abroad*

Sid James fell victim to a practical joke in Slough, where all the travel agency scenes were shot. After talking to the travel agent, he was simply meant to pick up his case and leave. At rehearsals the case was light because it was empty, but for the actual filming, the prop crew had filled it up with breeze blocks. James said his lines and right on cue went out to reach for his case and nearly pulled his arm out of its socket, much to the mirth of the assembled crew.

While filming at the travel agency in Slough, a real travel agent stormed into the shop that was being used, demanding to know why his rival was able to afford to charge such ridiculous rates for trips abroad. It was gently pointed out to him that in reality the shop was being used as a film set and the prices had all been made up!

After playing several supporting roles in the past few *Carry On*s, Peter Butterworth came back with an outlandish performance playing Pepe, the owner of the hotel in Elsbels. The film's finale involved him trying to desperately stop the kitchens from flooding, and he had quite a bit of difficulty in filming this. 'The kitchen has all these red tiles over it,' he recalled, 'and when water was pumped on to them the whole thing turned into a skating rink. It was like walking on ice. Gerald Thomas was in hysterics watching me trying to get across

Brother Bernard with Brother Martin (Derek Francis)

The tour party arrives at their hotel in Elsbels

the room and block the hole from where the water was leaking, and he said to me afterwards that he didn't realise I was such an acrobat. The *Carry On*s did occasionally have a habit of turning into death traps!'

The hotel exterior was built on the studio backlot at Pinewood, with truckloads of sand being brought in to make the immediate area look like a beach. The problem was that whilst everybody was lying around, rubbing suntan lotion on each other, in reality the weather was extremely cold. Bresslaw remembered Hawtrey's

antics on that set: 'Charles had to come out in these skimpy trunks and do his normal "Oh hello!" routine while looking as though he was having a wonderful time. We were all freezing cold but he was fine and seemed totally oblivious to the chill factor. During the lunch break I went over to his dressing room to see if he would tell me what his secret was. There was no answer when I knocked on the door but I could hear a noise, so I stuck my head around the door. There was Charles, napping in a chair with an empty bottle of rum in the bin beside him. No wonder he had looked so happy!'

A gap of one year followed *Carry On Abroad*, during which time Rogers and

Thomas turned their attentions to making a film adaptation of Sid James's highly successful TV sitcom *Bless This House*, using several of the *Carry On* regulars in supporting roles. The writer was Dave Freeman, who would eventually take over writing the *Carry On* scripts from Talbot Rothwell.

In September 1973 location filming for *Carry On Girls* began in Brighton. This film was Rothwell's parody on the seaside beauty contests that seemed to dominate such resorts. 'I have had the misfortune of seeing those dreadful end-of-pier glamour shows where you invariably get overweight women in minute bikinis, proudly displaying all that they possess on high heels. I remember that in the contest I saw, the compère was called Freddie Frolicker, which goes to show you the kind of level that these things reached.

During the press interviews for *Carry On Girls*, Sid James spoke

about how he thought the *Carry On* films were more than just a normal comedy series. '*Carry On* is now part of the language, because I've been told on countless occasions about incidents

Barbara Windsor poses with a Ferrari for *Carry On Girls* publicity

Margaret Nolan Valerie Leon and Babs

where people have had things happen to them and they've said, "It was so *Carry On*." To tell the truth, things have happened to me where I've thought that it was just like a *Carry On* film as well. If it ever ends up in the dictionary, I think it should have an explanation running along the lines of "bizarre series of humorous events strung together by happy accidents". When we were in Brighton filming *Girls* an old woman came up to me laughing herself silly and said that she only had to look at me and she immediately thought of someone with a daffodil sticking out of their backside. I didn't even bother telling her that I wasn't in that one, but I think I knew what she meant.'

Kenneth Connor had a worrying moment during an afternoon's filming at a fire station, where a sequence was staged which required his trousers to be torn off, having been caught up on a departing fire engine's rear. Connor explained what his problem had been: 'The costume people had made these trousers specially so that they would tear away quite easily, but I think they must have been trying to frighten me to death, because one of them came up and said that it would be best to brace myself when the fire engine pulled away, as if the driver mistimed the take, certain parts of my

anatomy would also come away with the trousers! I made the mistake of asking what would happen if the fire engine moved a fraction slower. I was told that if the initial force didn't get me, then the friction burns certainly would. I think you can see my knees knocking on the finished film, and that part certainly wasn't due to good or realistic acting. It was out of sheer terror!'

Bresslaw had to don a dress for the second film in a row, and was far happier about the quality of the clothes in this *Carry On*. 'I was quite glamorous in *Carry On Girls*; I

Connor loses his trousers yet again

**A great publicity stunt - but chaos ensued when
the donkey disgraced himself on the carpet**

was even given one of those lift and separate
bras! I dread to think what bust size they
gave me! My real problem was that I have
an inability to coordinate my feet whenever
it comes to wearing flowing robes or dresses
and the problem was even worse in this film
as I had to wear high heels as well. Sid
James was winding me up continually,
groping my rear and blowing me kisses,
saying, "Bernie, you look lovely, fancy a
quick drink? Your room or mine?"

As with every other *Carry On* film Bresslaw
appeared in, he managed to get the phrase 'I

only asked' in at some point during the
story. This was a huge in-joke that Rothwell
in particular tried to maintain, and Bresslaw
revealed why: 'It's all because of *The Army
Game*, where I played Private 'Popeye'
Popplewell. It was my catchphrase during
that series and I even made a record called
'I Only Asked'. Talbot wrote it into every
Carry On film as an affectionate nod to the
past, and as far as I know, that line was
never cut out at the editing stage.'

Rothwell was keen to try his hand at
another historical *Carry On*, following on
from the batch of contemporary films that
had been made since *Carry On Henry*. The
legend of Dick Turpin seemed like an ideal

topic, and with the approval of Thomas and Rogers, he started to draft the screenplay while they were filming *Carry On Girls* in

'Fill my glass right up or I'll blow your nose off!'

Brighton. It was while working on the new script that something very strange and frightening happened to him, as Rothwell detailed: 'I think I must have been working on the last twenty minutes or so of the film;

An unsuccessful hold up?

had headed for my typewriter, and that's when the problem began. The keys became a puzzle and it was almost as if I couldn't register what they were or what you had to do with them to get the typewriter to work. It wasn't as though I couldn't come up with the dialogue or jokes, because I had spent most of the morning thinking them up. I just couldn't physically coordinate myself to be able to type. My hands were on the keys but my brain just wouldn't let me do the rest of it.

'I ended up getting my daughter Jane in on the act. I dictated from my notes and she just typed the whole thing up. I went to the doctor just as soon as I could and he told me it was all due to eye-strain and exhaustion. His advice was to take a long, long break from writing. It was as though my brain and body were out

it was a case of tidying up the finale and coming up with a punchline. I had got up that morning, had a healthy breakfast and

Hello boys!

traditional cast.

Sid James had allegedly grown tired of the growing level of smut in each film, and with *Bless This House* on television taking up so much of his time, he felt that there was not that much to lose by backing out of the films. Barbara Windsor also wanted to move on to other projects, and *Dick* marked her last appearance in the regular films, although she did return to co-host

Williams looks on as Jack Douglas gets the bird in *Carry On Dick*

of sync and I had to stop before it was too late.'

This problem meant that *Carry On Dick* was the last script that Rothwell would write for Rogers and Peters for the big screen. He had been credited as the writer of every *Carry On* film since *Carry On Cabby*, the sole exception being *Carry On Spying* which he co-wrote with Sid Colin. As it would turn out, *Carry On Dick* was a throwback to the good old funny days, and it was also the last film to feature several members of the

the compilation film *That's Carry On*, and, like James, she had no qualms about taking part in *Carry On Laughing*, the series of half-hour comedies that were made for Thames Television in 1974 and 1975. James was certainly more than happy to acknowledge the place that the *Carry On* films had in both his affections and career, as he said after *Carry On Dick* went out on general release: 'There are two things above anything else that I would cite as being the best things that ever happened to me as far as my career is concerned, and that was working on the radio and television versions of *Hancock's Half Hour* and all of the *Carry*

In *Carry On Dick*, Penny Irving (above) played one of the Birds of Paradise and Hattie Jacques myseriously shrank to less than three feet tall

March 1974, both James and Windsor were spending their days in front of the cameras and their evenings on stage at the Victoria Palace Theatre in London, where *Carry On London* was enjoying an immensely successful run, having opened for Christmas 1973. It was basically a variety show starring all the regular cast members, with the exception of Kenneth Williams, who declined the offer to participate. The revue was loved by audiences and critics alike, and the whole project raked in a small fortune at the box-office.

On films that I've been in. Both had their ups and downs, but if you asked me whether I'd do it all again, the answer would be yes. I've made more friends on the *Carry Ons* and shared more laughs with them than I would ever even hope to remember and I don't regret a minute of it. It is, however, time to move on.'

While *Carry On Dick* was being filmed in

111

began to feel the effects of the cold spring weather.

'Sid James and his gang had to rob the coach that Margaret Nolan and I were travelling in, and the whole point of the gag was that the outlaws stole everything from us, even the clothes we were dressed in, bar our shoes and hats. Well, I was a little worried as to how much my hat would cover and poor Mags must have felt the same. I went over to Gerald and said, "About the hat for the forest scene..." but before I could say anything else he just looked at me and said, "Who said anything about the hat? Haven't you read the rewrite?" I said that I hadn't and he said, "Well, Dick Turpin just leaves you with a handkerchief and even that blows away in the wind. Remember Babs and the bikini in *Carry On Camping*? Well, we've got the same guy with the fishing line and he's coming along to yank the thing away on cue." Well, that chilled my blood, as you can imagine!

They said it with borrowed flowers when Barbara Windsor returned to *Carry On London* after injuring her back

'When we got to the woods I found out that I had been subjected to one of Gerald's most malicious wind-ups because there was a huge hat as part of my costume and Mags also had an enormous hat. It was then Gerald pulled his masterstroke. "Knickers as well, Bernard!" he called, and when I

The forest sequences in *Carry On Dick* were staged at Black Park and Windsor Great Park, while the streets of London were reconstructed at Pinewood. It was during one of the woodland scenes where Bresslaw protested he told me that if they got a flash of my hips, it was no good seeing Y-fronts as they hadn't been invented back then. So, while he let Mags keep all her underwear on, the only thing I was allowed to wear was my pair of shoes, and when the wind whistles in Windsor Great Park, it really does whistle! I can't tell you where I got icicles, but you probably don't want to know!'

Carry On Dick marked the last appearance in the *Carry On* series by Hattie Jacques, who had been in fourteen films since *Carry On Sergeant*. It was quite clear that with all the old guard disappearing, a whole batch of new stars would have to be brought in before work on the next film could begin.

Jacques died in 1980 and Williams paid tribute to her work in the films. 'Hattie was bracketed with myself, Sid James, Bernard Bresslaw, Kenny Connor and Charles Hawtrey as being part of "Gerald's Old Retainers", in that if

one or two of us were absent from a film, the rest of us would be there. From Hattie's death onwards, it didn't really feel as though we were making 'proper' *Carry On*s any more. I missed Hattie in particular because

It's a good job berets weren't in fashion back then

The lovely Valerie (Jenny Cox) meets Professors Crump and Vooshka in _Carry On Behind_

a stupid ass of a costume girl got me into the wrong costume and Gerald went spare, complaining that the light was fading fast and that the shot would be ruined if I didn't speed up and get changed. I tried to placate him, offering him some choice words of poetry, but he just yelled at me: "We're not here to shoot poetry, we're here to shoot shit!", and when I saw the finished film, I couldn't help but agree with his sentiments.'

With _Bless This House_ film writer Dave Freeman moving into Talbot Rothwell's shoes, work began on _Carry On Behind_, which centred on an archeological dig for some rude Roman mosaics at an old caravan site. As with _Carry On Camping_, the orchard at Pinewood was duly touched up with green paint once again to make the place resemble a caravan park at the height of summer rather than a muddy orchard in wintry March. And, just to repeat history, many of the scenes featured bikini-clad women who in reality were shivering with cold rather than basking in the summer heat.

In amongst many of the new faces Rogers and Thomas had cast, including TV stars such as Windsor Davies and Ian Lavender, was the popular European actress Elke

we'd worked together for so long and so often, but every time I wanted to pop into her dressing room for a chat I'd have to pull back and remember that she wasn't there any more.'

Williams also carried a more cynical memory of _Carry On Dick_: 'I remember that

Sommer. The reason for casting her in a leading role was to attract audiences in Germany and France, where her work was more widely known. She was paired off against Williams, who went out of his way to bring her into the family fold. At the time he explained why he felt this was so important: 'Elke was delightful, positively enchanting, and I have to admit that I went out of my way to make her welcome,

Bottom's up! One of the publicity shots for
Carry On Behind

because the poor girl was terrified at the prospect of working with the likes of myself, Kenny Connor and Bernard, because we'd been together for so long and she felt like an intruder. It must have been a little under a week before she settled, and I think it was the sausage story that broke the ice.

'Gerald used to love tormenting the male actors, who had read the script and were positively enthralled at the prospect of having to ogle some young near-naked beauty. The shock would then come on set, when they found out that Gerald had

already shot all the scenes he needed of the young girls and all he needed now were the actors' lecherous reactions. He honestly seemed to take some malicious pleasure in standing there and saying, "Look at my boobs! They're so round and bouncy!" just to get them going. Well, the sausage came into it because the actors were told beforehand to practise leching, and the best way to do that was to lech at their dinner. So, you'd occasionally see an actor in the canteen, flirting with a sausage at the end of his fork.'

After spending much of the beginning of the year working on the *Carry On Laughing*

Jack Douglas, Windsor Davies and Kenneth Connor in *Carry On Behind* - staring at a sausage?

series at Thames Television Studios, Kenneth Connor found the contrast of going back to the film series quite a shock: 'One moment you were in the warmth of the television studios and in the next, you were out there in that damned orchard with the props guys trying to spray the frost in the trees with paint to make them look like blossoms. The mud was so thick that you were in real danger of sinking up to your waist if you didn't keep on moving. You felt as though you were in a remake of *Sanders of the River* and a crocodile would glide past at any second. It went from snow to rain, with the occasional brief hint of sunshine, before it began snowing again.

'I remember the press call day, because Gerald and Peter came up with the idea of having a line of girls with holes in the seat of their jeans. They could all then stand in line, cheek to cheek if you will, and turn to the cameras and smile happily. The idea was to emphasise the *Carry On Behind* title. In the end the pictures looked all right because they were printed in the papers in black and white. If they'd been in colour you would have seen that the girls' buttocks were actually blue and frozen from the cold!'

Unlike the highly

Captain S. Melly and Sergeant Major Bloomer sound the alarm in *Carry On England*

popular *Carry On Dick, Carry On Behind* was not a success, although the trick of employing Elke Sommer did pay off in Europe. *Behind* was one of the more popular *Carry On*s in France and Germany, just as hoped.

In the following spring it was announced that *Carry On England* was the title of the 27th *Carry On* in 18 years. The series had now come full circle - the first one, *Carry On Sergeant*, had been set in the grounds of army barracks and so would *Carry On England*. *England* was, however, targeted at a far more adult audience than any of its predecessors.

The *Confessions* films, starring *Carry On Girls* actor Robin Asquith, had started to appear in the early 1970s, and their mixture of soft-core porn and raucous comedy proved to be hugely popular with cinema-going audiences. It was only logical for the *Carry On* films to try and compete.

Up until that point, the *Carry On*s had only hinted at sex; a bare breast was occasionally flashed on screen. *Carry On England* went way beyond that, with Jack Seddon's and David Purcell's script using sex as the main motivation behind many of the characters' antics. The film included one scene where an entire squad of women from the anti-aircraft battery march topless

The uniform would fall off, but Gerald Thomas makes sure that the moustache stays on

on the parade ground. It was this scene which led to the film being given an AA certificate by the censors, ensuring that it would lose a vast majority of the younger audiences which the films were so popular with.

Peter Butterworth was one of the few long term *Carry On* actors who was present in this film. He commented after the film's release that he had found the whole thing a strange experience that was lacking in real comedy: 'Everyone had gone, and I was only there for a couple of days, but there was no Sid, no Hattie, no Kenneth Williams, no Bernard Bresslaw, just myself and Kenneth

Connor. The whole thing didn't have the energy of the earlier films and there was just no real sense of fun. The jokes were smutty more than funny and as a consequence the film suffered. To be honest, I thought the whole thing was a real shame.'

Connor once again went through the process of having to lose his clothes on screen. During a march, which his character, Captain S. Melly, is leading, his sabotaged uniform drops to bits, with

sections falling off every hundred yards. Connor told of the panic that set in when filming that scene: 'Bits were being yanked off by wires, and the whole thing was only held together by a wing and a prayer. I was almost afraid to move when they put me into it in case a cough or sneeze did irreparable damage to the uniform. Anyway, when it got down to the last bit that was meant to fall off, I felt the wire catch the

turned to blind panic and that's why I look as though I've got something wrong with my legs in the film. I was trying to stride out and free my shorts a the same time, and by some miracle, it actually worked and my dignity remained intact.'

The only *Carry On* of any note during the next few years involved a single day's filming on *That's*

underwear I had on underneath, and I could slowly feel my pants edging down around my waist. Not only would all the actors behind me have gotten an eyeful of the Connor posterior, the Connor crown jewels would have ended up on display in front of the camera lens, recorded on film for posterity. As you can imagine, mild panic

Claire Davenport floors Kenneth Connor and Suzanne Danielle does the same for Williams in *Carry On Emanuelle*

Carry On, a compilation of clips hosted by Kenneth Williams and Barbara Windsor. The shoot took place on 12 July 1977 in a projection booth at Pinewood Studios. Williams feelings on the matter were very strong: 'If anything, it made you realise how the films had lost their way. Looking at the old clips brought it all back, and one saw how truthful and clear the comedy in many of Talbot Rothwell's early scripts were. If anything, the whole experience made me long for the past.'

Carry On Laughing

Cinema audiences seemed to agree with Williams. *That's Carry On* did far better than *Carry On England*. Its success was enough to make Peter Rogers decide to go ahead with his plan of putting together a series of compilation-clip programmes for television, which in turn became highly popular and are constantly being repeated.

If sex had been the underlying theme of *Carry On England*, then the title alone of the next one was enough to betray its whole tone. *Carry On Emmanuelle* sent up the pornographic film series which had been a hit both in England and on the continent and had made a star of its leading lady, Sylvia Kristel.

Extensive casting to find a bright new actress to play the lead role got underway at the beginning of 1978, with Rogers and Thomas finally choosing Suzanne Danielle, who Kenneth Williams took an immediate shine to when shooting began in the second week of April that year. Much of the script involved him having to bare his rear whilst in various compromising positions with Danielle. 'Suzanne is a delight to work with,' he said at the time when post-filming

Jim Dale returned as Columbus for his first *Carry On* in 23 years - Julian Clary savours the moment

publicity was hitting the papers. 'I think there is more talent there than you'd find in many young actresses today. She has grace and charm and is also extremely attractive. It was a pleasure to work with her.'

Five years later on Williams spoke more bluntly about the film, though his praise of

Connor, however, did have one amusing anecdote from *Carry On Emmanuelle*. 'Gerald staged a scene where I got dragged into the bedroom by a formidable actress called Claire Davenport. We practised the moves in rehearsal of her grabbing my collar and dragging me inside, and that was fine, but when we did it for real, she grabbed me really hard and I was suddenly on the floor. She was just so strong that it completely caught me unawares. I thought I had all the stuffing knocked out of me but Gerald just kept filming and only called "cut!" when he thought he had all he needed!'

Like *Carry On Behind* and *Carry On England*, *Carry On Emmanuelle* did not perform well at the box-office. The film had been made with a new investment company as by then Rogers had parted company with Rank, feeling that the organisation was not promoting the new *Carry On* films strongly enough. The new company, however, refused to put up financing for the next film that was being planned, *Carry On Again Nurse*. This proposed sixth medical *Carry On* was to have brought back as many of the original team as possible. Charles Hawtrey would have been given a lead role, together with Windsor taking the female lead, but it was not to be.

the actress remained undimmed. 'The script left a lot to be desired,' he said, 'and I have to admit that I found many of the jokes quite repulsive. Perhaps my definition of comedy is at odds with current trends, but I just believe that to gain the sympathy of the audience for your character, you have to maintain a sense of reality, no matter how fantastical the situation becomes. Maybe I realised that this film was the death knell for the series, which is why my attitude towards it is as it is.'

Despite other scripts being written during the course of the 1980s, like *Carry On Down Under*, with finance possibly coming from an Australian backer, or *Carry On Dallas*, with

Kenneth Williams pencilled in to play a character based on the popular soap opera's villain J. R. Ewing, renamed R. U. Screwing, nothing ever came to fruition.

A new decade opened with new plans to revive the *Carry On* series. John Goldstone had worked as a producer on such hits as *Monty Python's Life of Brian* and saw immense potential in dusting off the *Carry On* franchise to film a parody of the Christopher Columbus epics that were being prepared for 1992 in celebration of the 500th anniversary of the discovery of America. With *Christopher Columbus - The Discovery* and Ridley Scott's *1492* well underway, *Carry On Columbus* would be a spoof on them in much the same way *Carry On Cleo* had been on *Cleopatra* and *Carry On Henry* had been on *Anne of a Thousand Days*.

With financing secured from Island World Films, working alongside Goldstone's own company, Comedy House Productions, many of the old behind-the-scenes crew were brought back to work on the first *Carry On* for fifteen years. Gerald Thomas would once again be in the director's chair while Peter Rogers acted as executive producer. The script would be written by *Carry On Behind*'s writer, Dave Freeman, but the question which remained unresolved was how many of the original stars would want to return in this venture.

The sad fact of the matter was that many of the *Carry On* regulars had passed away. Sid James, Hattie Jacques, Charles Hawtrey, Kenneth Connor, Peter Butterworth and Kenneth Williams had all died by 1992, while survivors like Barbara Windsor and Joan Sims felt that they didn't wish to be involved.

In the intervening years since *Carry On Again Doctor*, Jim Dale had gone on to work to great acclaim at the National Theatre before moving to America, where he had become a huge star on Broadway, playing the lead in such shows as *Barnum!* and *Me and My Girl*. When he was approached to play the lead role of Christopher Columbus, he was only too happy to say yes.

Many of the semi-regulars also returned, with Bernard Cribbins, Jon Pertwee, Jack Douglas, June Whitfield and Leslie Philips amongst their number. One thing that hadn't changed was the production schedule, with only six weeks of shooting planned to be carried out from the beginning of April 1992. With a host of young comedians also on board, such as Rik Mayall, Nigel Planer, Julian Clary and Alexei Sayle, the *Carry On* series was back, much to the delight of Rogers and Thomas. As filming got underway, Dale commented on how strange it felt to be back at Pinewood some 20 years after his last visit: 'It's strange because so many of the old gang are gone now, but I feel as though their ghosts are all around the set. It's almost as though you expect to hear Kenneth Williams' voice still ringing down the corridors. I miss them not being here ... all of them.'

Another aspect of the film that hadn't changed since the old days was the lack of exotic location work. Although in real life Columbus had discovered the New World, the cast and crew of *Columbus* found themselves in a flooded sandpit for several days. When shooting finished, the level of press interest and public expectation was extreme. The film was perceived as being like an old friend returning from the past,

Rik Mayall gives a word of advice to Bert Kwouk watched by Nigel Planer

and everyone was eager to be reunited again.

Sadly this was not to be the case. Although public enthusiasm was high, the critical reaction was bloodthirsty, with many stating that the *Carry On* films should have been left as they were and not been brought kicking and screaming into the 1990s. Nostalgic fans, however, lapped up every minute of it.

Following on from *Columbus* there was a press rumour that a second new film, provisionally titled *Carry On Buddha*, was in the pipeline, but no such script seems to have been ever commissioned. Today, Peter Rogers is optimistic that there is still life in the series and that the format could be adapted for television, but the style would never be the same again as sadly, Gerald Thomas recently passed away.

In terms of production and crew, an entire new team would have to take over, with Rogers at the helm, but let us not forget that we still have the original 31 films to enjoy, with every one of them regularly turning up on television and the home video market. Although so many of the original *Carry On* stars are no longer here, people are still discovering the delights of the films and one thing is clear: they, and the *Carry On* films, will certainly never be forgotten.

Carry On Chronology

or

Everything You've Ever Wanted to Know about the Carry On Lists but Couldn't be Bothered to Ask

INTRODUCTION

Up to 1995 there is a grand total of thirty entries in the Carry On series. If you want to be a bit of a know-all and point out that there was a compilation film called *That's Carry On* in 1977 then the total becomes thirty-one.

In the following chronology, apart from a brief synopsis and notes on the cast and crew for each film, there's a brief critique which is based solely on the author's opinion, so don't go complaining to the publishers!

CARRY ON SERGEANT

1958

'Your rank?'
'That's a matter of opinion!'

It's the time when national service was still compulsory in this land and a platoon of servicemen with the military potential of a one-legged stoat have been allocated to the bombastic Sergeant Grimshaw, who is on the verge of retirement. He has placed a substantial bet with his fellow sergeants that he can get his men through training with flying colours and win the Star Squad prize - he wants to go out in a blaze of glory! His men, however, don't know their bayonets from their bellybuttons but pull out all the stops when they find out how much is riding on their success and start behaving more like soldiers, much to Grimshaw's surprise and disbelief.

Familiar Faces

William Hartnell: Television's first Doctor Who, who was in the role from 1963 to 1966.

Bob Monkhouse: Comedy deity of the highest order.

Bill Owen: Now Compo in *Last of the Summer Wine*.

Shirley Eaton: Legendary gold-painted victim in *Goldfinger*.

Jack Smethurst: Later the star of that not very PC sitcom, *Love Thy Neighbour*. Chalky, indeed!

Gerald Campion: Forever remembered as the fat schoolboy Billy Bunter.

Henry Livings: Later a playwright of some repute.

The Verdict

A typical service comedy, very much in the style of the farces being produced towards the end of the 1950s, when the Ealing Comedy classics had all but died out and everybody else was trying to live up to their

Bob Monkhouse with Kenneth Connor (above) and Shirley Eaton (left) in his only *Carry On* film.

formidable reputation. There are none of the innuendo-laden scenes that audiences would come to expect, but the verbal puns are certainly present and correct. Essentially, *Carry On Sergeant* was the embryonic form of what was destined to follow, and the actors who would go on to become regular performers in the series are all on form and noticeably very young looking when compared to their appearances only a few years later. Monkhouse is perfectly at ease and it's a shame that this was his only appearance in a *Carry On* film.

Cast list

Sergeant Grimshaw	William Hartnell
Charlie Sage	Bob Monkhouse
Mary	Shirley Eaton
Captain Potts	Eric Barker
Nora	Dora Bryan
Corporal Copping	Bill Owen
Horace Strong	Kenneth Connor
Peter Golightly	Charles Hawtrey
James Bailey	Kenneth Williams
Miles Heywood	Terence Longden
Herbert Brown	Norman Rossington
Captain Clark	Hattie Jacques
Andy Galloway	Gerald Campion
First Recruit	Jack Smethurst
Thirteenth Recruit	Henry Livings

Crew list

Written by Norman Hudis, based on *The Bull Boys* by R. F. Delderfield
Additional material   John Antrobus
Music   Bruce Montgomery
Music played by The Band of the Coldstream Guards
Cinematographer   Peter Hennessy
Art Director   Alex Vetchinsky
Producer   Peter Rogers
Director   Gerald Thomas

Certificate U (black and white)   **Running time: approx. 83 minutes**

Carry On Nurse

'Come, come, Matron. Surely you've seen a temperature taken like this before?'
'Yes, Colonel, many times ... but never with a daffodil!'

The patients in Haven Hospital, and particularly the residents in the men's ward, all wilt under the domineering rule of their imposing matron. Bernie Bishop is a kind-hearted boxer with a broken fist, Oliver Reckitt is a nuclear physicist and the crotchety Colonel is a racehorse-obsessed gambler. Along with their fellow bed-bound inmates, their stay reaches breaking point as far as facing hospital bureaucracy is concerned, and they decide that the time has come to do something about it. As night falls, a carefully planned covert operation is put into action by the rebelling patients.

Familiar Faces

Wilfrid Hyde-White: Famous character actor who appeared in such films as *The Third Man*.

Jill Ireland: Future Hollywood star; then the wife of David McCallum. She later tied the knot with Charles Bronson.

Joan Hickson: The BBC's definitive Miss Marple.

Irene Handl: Popular comedy actress who was later the sparring partner of Metal Mickey (remember him?).

Michael Medwin: Popular film actor of the 1950s who later moved into film production yet still made an appearance on the other side of the camera as Eddie Shoestring's boss in *Shoestring*.

The Verdict

Widely regarded as one of the best *Carry On* films, although in retrospect it clearly hadn't reached the

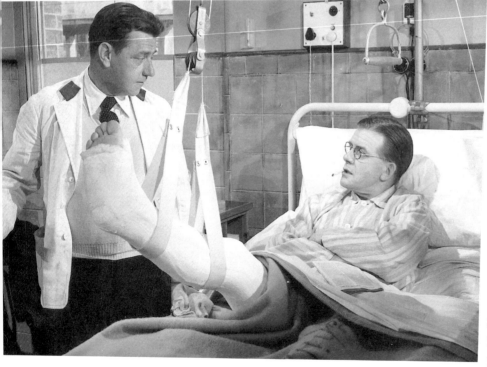

Bill Owen smoking in hospital and plastered too!

heights of invention that the later bedpan farces would achieve. There are signs of things to come - the daffodil gag is just one memorable example.

Hattie Jacques is almost a prototype of the matron who would emerge in *Carry On Doctor*, where Kenneth Williams would move out of his role as a patient, as he is here, and become her sparring partner in *Doctor* and all of the other medical titles in the series. Like *Carry On Sergeant*, the film's roots as a stage play do betray themselves

every so often, but the enterprise as a whole is immense fun and it's clear that by this film the groundwork which made the franchise run for so long has been firmly laid.

Three-year-old Jeremy Connor visited his dad at work and became a film star! He was signed up to play - what else - Connor's son.

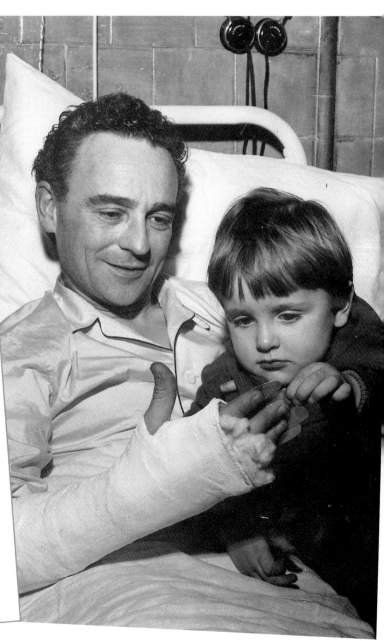

Cast list

Dorothy Denton	Shirley Eaton
Bernie Bishop	Kenneth Connor
Hinton	Charles Hawtrey
Matron	Hattie Jacques
Ted York	Terence Longden
Percy Hickson	Bill Owen
Jack Bell	Leslie Philips
Stella Dawson	Joan Sims
Georgie Axwell	Susan Stephen
Oliver Reckitt	Kenneth Williams
The Colonel	Wilfrid Hyde-White
Frances James	Susan Beaumont
Norm	Norman Rossington
Jill Thompson	Jill Ireland
Sister	Joan Hickson
Helen Lloyd	Ann Firbank
Mrs Marge Hickson	Irene Handl
Mrs Jane Bishop	Susan Shaw
Ginger	Michael Medwin

Crew list

Written by Norman Hudis, based on an idea by Patrick Cargill and Jack Searle

Music	Bruce Montgomery
Cinematography	Reg Wyer, BSC
Art Director	Alex Vetchinsky
Producer	Peter Rogers
Director	Gerald Thomas

Certificate U (black and white)   Running time: approx. 86 minutes

Carry On Teacher

1959

'Are you satisfied with your equipment, Miss Allcock?'
'Well! I've had no complaints so far.'

Normally, a headmaster's application to move on to another school would run along a smooth course of bureaucracy, but not so for William Wakefield, who severely underestimates his popularity with the pupils of Maudlin Street School. In fact, they are determined to ensure that he stays on. The results of schoolboy cunning are soon unearthed - the staffroom's supply of tea is laced with booze, Wakefield's study becomes infested with itching powder and finally the school is subjected to a bomb scare. However, the question remains whether the headmaster will find out about his boys' devotion, and when he does, will he be willing to stay on?

Familiar Faces

Ted Ray: Immensely popular comedy star of both radio and television from the 1940s onwards.

Richard O'Sullivan: Future star of sitcoms such as *Man About the House* and *Robin's Nest*, seen here as a child actor.

Carol White: Actress who would go on to play the lead in the legendary BBC play, *Cathy Come Home*, with films such as *Poor Cow* following on from that.

Larry Dann: Child actor who would go on to play one of the lead roles in *Carry On Emmanuelle* twenty years later. Now a regular on *The Bill*.

The Verdict

The first original storyline developed for the series is a bit of a curate's egg; some of the humour is straight out of the pages of *Billy Bunter* and influenced by the style of teacher/pupil antics borrowed from the *St Trinian* films while other parts were more 'straight' and would re-emerge years later in the television sitcom *Please Sir!* The regular cast were by now all beginning to hit their stride and work well together, and Ted Ray

Cast list

William Wakefield	Ted Ray
Gregory Adams	Kenneth Connor
Michael Bean	Charles Hawtrey
Alistair Grigg	Leslie Philips
Sarah Allcock	Joan Sims
Edwin Milton	Kenneth Williams
Grace Short	Hattie Jacques
Felicity Wheeler	Rosalind Knight
Alf	Cyril Chamberlain
Robin Stevens	Richard O'Sullivan
Sheila Dale	Carol White
Boy	Larry Dunn

Crew list

Written by	Norman Hudis
Music	Bruce Montgomery
Cinematography	Reg Wyer, BSC
Art Director	Lionel Couch
Producer	Peter Rogers
Director	Gerald Thomas

Certificate **U** (black and white) **Running time:** approx. 86 minutes

Itching powder drove them mad in the head's study (above) but the only thing they want to scratch in the staffroom (right) is each other's eyes out!

is fine as the lead. *Carry On Teacher* does not feel like a generic *Carry On* film, yet at the same time it could hardly be anything else.

CARRY ON CONSTABLE

'Look in on Mrs Bottomley at number 24. She's complaining of suspicious activities in the rear of her premises.'

I t's useless recruit time once again as four trainee officers are put under the supervision of Sergeant Wilkins at his police station. It's clear he doesn't think they'll survive long enough to collect their pensions but wearily tries to do what he can with them. Robbers are assisted instead of arrested, old ladies are dragged, protesting, across the road and a brilliant idea to act as store detectives in drag goes horribly wrong as the pair of constables responsible for the

brainwave are themselves arrested. As always, the chance comes for them to redeem themselves as the trainees join forces to hunt down a wage-snatching gang.

Familiar Faces

Freddie Mills: Famous boxer whose untimely death has long been the subject of press speculation.

Esma Cannon: Diminutive character actress, known for her appearance in ITV's *The Rag Trade* in the early 1960s.

Noel Dyson: Loved as Nanny in the long-running television sitcom *Father, Dear Father*.

Robin Ray: Son of Ted Ray; later became a broadcaster on TV and radio on the subjects of classical music and the history of cinema.

Cast list

Sergeant Frank Wilkins	Sid James
Inspector Mills	Eric Barker
Constable Charlie Constable	Kenneth Connor
Special Constable Gorse	Charles Hawtrey
Constable Benson	Kenneth Williams
Constable Potter	Leslie Philips
WPC Gloria Passworthy	Joan Sims
Sergeant Laura Moon	Hattie Jacques
Sally	Shirley Eaton
Constable Thurston	Cyril Chamberlain
Mrs May	Joan Hickson
Distraught woman	Irene Handl
Herbert Hall	Terence Longden
Harrison	Jill Adams
First crook	Freddie Mills
Deaf old woman	Esma Cannon
Vague woman	Noel Dyson
Assistant Manager	Robin Ray

Crew list

Written by Norman Hudis, based on an idea by Brock Williams	
Music	Bruce Montgomery
Cinematographer	Ted Scaife, BSC
Art Director	Carmen Dillon
Producer	Peter Rogers
Director	Gerald Thomas

Certificate U (black and white) Running time: approx. 86 minutes

Special Constable Gorse's bird is behind bars down at the local nick.

The Verdict

A strange hybrid of the kind of comedies that Will Hay used to make in the 1930s and 1940s, several of which had featured the very young Charles Hawtrey. Although the style of knockabout humour was becoming firmly established, *Carry On Constable* is perhaps the least popular of the early films. It seems very dated and slightly eccentric now, but there are still many moments to cherish, such as the naked shower sequence and Hawtrey and William's drag act. Sid James makes an assured debut and fits in well with the rest of the established team. It's quite clear from his performance that knockabout comedy suits his style, and Rogers would have been foolish if he'd allowed this to be James's sole performance in the series.

More than just their truncheons would be on display in the infamous shower scene.

Carry On Regardless

'Please, don't make it hard for me.'
'I'm finding it a bit hard already … to understand.'

The Helping Hands Agency takes on six unemployed men and women and one of the clerks at the labour exchange who decides to join them in their quest for an exciting job. The six of them find themselves undertaking a very odd series of assignments, which range from taking a chimp for a day out, trying to stay sober at a wine tasting and demonstrating new pieces of equipment at the Ideal Home Exhibition. Naturally, everything they put their hands to goes terribly wrong.

Familiar Faces

Fenella Fielding: Camp icon and Marty Feldman's sister, who would later star in *Carry On Screaming*.

Stanley Unwin: Practically the inventor of gobbledegook, which made for many various TV and film appearances.

Terence Alexander: Later familiar as Charlie Hungerford in the long-running BBC series *Bergerac*.

The incomparable Hattie Jacques.

Norman Rossington: One of the regular cast of *The Army Game*.

Jerry Desmond: Double act partner of the legendary Sid Field.

Nicholas Parsons: One-time stooge to the late Arthur Haines and the host with the most on Anglia's *Sale of the Century*.

Patrick Cargill: Popular actor, forever remembered as the father in *Father, Dear Father*.

The Verdict

The problem with *Carry On Regardless* is that there is no real plot as such, but a series of sketches which are all loosely tied in together with the link of the Helping Hands Agency. Some of the sketches are real hits while others miss by a long mark. The cast regulars are all on top form and there is an unusual number of familiar faces in supporting roles. *Carry On Regardless* is the perfect example of Norman Hudis's writing, where a group of characters share the same problem and then come together to solve it. It's a strange film and some may argue that there is no real sense of direction, but it cannot be denied that it was a major step forward towards the kind of anarchy which was to come later on.

The spray came from out of the picture, not from Sid James.

Cast list

Bert Handy	Sid James
Sam Twist	Kenneth Connor
Gabriel Dimple	Charles Hawtrey
Lily Duveen	Joan Sims
Francis Courtney	Kenneth Williams
Mike Weston	Bill Owen
Delia King	Liz Fraser
Montgomery Infield-Hopping	Terence Longden
Penny Panting	Fenella Fielding
Miss Cooling	Esma Cannon
Matron	Hattie Jacques
Landlord	Stanley Unwin
Mrs Riley	Eleanor Summerfield
Mr Panting	Ed Devereaux
Park keeper	Cyril Chamberlain
Nursing sister	Joan Hickson
Trevor Trelawney	Terence Alexander
Referee	Norman Rossington
Club manager	Sydney Taffler
Martin Paul	Jerry Desmond
Wine 'Wolf'	Nicholas Parsons
Raffish customer	Patrick Cargill
Mata Hari	Betty Marsden
Bird woman	Molly Weir
Sinister man	Eric Pohlmann
Wine organiser	Howard Marion Crawford
Bus conductor	Tony Sagar
Young connoisseur	David Lodge
Massive Mickey McGee	Tom Clegg
Lefty	Freddie Mills

Crew list

Written by	Norman Hudis
Music	Bruce Montgomery
Cinematography	Alan Hume BSC
Art Director	Lionel Couch
Producer	Peter Rogers
Director	Gerald Thomas

Certificate **U** (black and white) **Running time:** approx. 90 minutes

CARRY ON CRUISING

1962

'A captain must understand his men so I'm going to use the psychological approach. I don't claim to be a Jung man ...'
'So long as you're young in heart, Sir.'

Captain Crowther attempts to board Flo Castle.

haos reigns on a Mediterranean cruise liner with a group of passengers on board who seem to be just as inept as most of the crew, who are under the command of the serious and uptight Captain Crowther. He has to contend with a hopelessly seasick chef, a First Officer who is the epitome of the word 'snooty' and the ship's doctor, who has fallen in love with one of the passengers. Things come to a climax when the crew plan a surprise party for the captain who is celebrating his tenth year at sea.

Familiar Faces
Lance Percival: One of the main participants of *That Was The Week That Was* in the early 1960s.
Anton Rodgers: Made his name in such musicals as *Pickwick* but best known for the sitcom *Fresh Fields* and its sequel *French Fields*.

The Verdict
Yet again, Hudis uses his tried and trusted trick of having a bunch of new recruits pitted against an authoritarian figure. This was his last script for the series, which also marked the first time a *Carry On* film was made in colour. Both Hawtrey and Jacques are noticeable by their absence, as is Joan Sims whose place is taken by Dilys Lane. Some scenes begin to verge on the raucous, especially where Williams and Connor are trying to inject Percival in his rear. One of the better films of that era, ranking alongside *Carry On Nurse* in quality.

Cast list

Captain Crowther	Sid James
First Officer Leonard Majorbanks	Kenneth Williams
Ship's Doctor Arthur Binn	Kenneth Connor
Glad Trimble	Liz Fraser
Flo Castle	Dilys Laye
Bridget Madderley	Esma Cannon
Chef Wilfred Haines	Lance Percival
Sam Turner	Jimmy Thompson
Drunk man	Ronnie Stephens
Jenkins	Vincent Ball
Tom Tree	Cyril Chamberlain
Very fat man	Willoughby Goddard
Young officer	Ed Devereaux
Steward	Brian Rawlinson
Young man	Anton Rodgers
First Cook	Anthony Sagar
Second Cook	Mario Fabrizi

Crew list

Written by	Norman Hudis, from a story by Eric Barker
Music	Bruce Montgomery & Douglas Gamely
Cinematography	Alan Hume BSC
Art Director	Carmen Dillon
Producer	Peter Rogers
Director	Gerald Thomas

Certificate U (colour) Running time: approx. 89 minutes

CARRY ON CABBY

'Don't laugh too much, you might strain something, and you don't want to wear one of them belts, do you?'
'I already do. The old woman gave it to me for Christmas.'
'That's what I like to see, a marriage based on mutual truss!'

The glamorous Anthea (Amanda Barrie) with the gormless Ted (Kenneth Connor).

The owner of Speedee Taxis is a certified workaholic, much to the increasing despair of his wife Peggy. Everything is forsaken for a fare, so Peggy decides it's time to do something about it; she'll show her beloved Charlie what stern stuff she's made of. Secretly with the wife of one of her husband's drivers, Peggy forms the exotic Glamcabs, and in so doing, practically steals all of Charlie's regular clients. He decides that the only course of action to take is to get one of his drivers 'on the inside' of Glamcabs and so sends in his best driver, Ted, disguised in fishnets and skirt to find out what it's all about!

Familiar Faces

Milo O'Shea: Renowned theatre and film actor, whose work has ranged from playing Bloom in the movie of Joyce's *Ulysses* to working with Paul Newman in *The Verdict*.

Amanda Barrie: Later the leading lady of *Carry On Cleo* and today better known as Alma, Mike Baldwin's wife in *Coronation Street*.

Peter Gilmore: Later the star of *The Onedin Line*, this was his first of many appearances in the *Carry On* films.

Peter Byrne: One of the stars of the long-running *Dixon of Dock Green*. In the early 1990s he was one of the lead actors in the sitcom *Bread*.

Glamcabs advertising hits home with Speedee Taxis.

The Verdict

Originally this film was not intended as part of the *Carry On* series. It's strange to see no sign of Williams but it's good to see the return of Hawtrey and Jacques. It's also strange to see that considering the sexist angle in most of the *Carry On* films, in this one it's the women who get the upper hand. The new scripting talents of Talbot Rothwell show the potential of what he eventually achieves with the films. There is more plot in this one than in any of its predecessors and it's fair to say that *Carry On Cabby* marked the beginning of a new era in the series, with a much faster pace of storytelling. This was Jacques' favourite *Carry On* film.

Cast list

Charlie	Sid James
Peggy	Hattie Jacques
Ted	Kenneth Connor
Pintpot	Charles Hawtrey
Flo	Esma Cannon
Sally	Liz Fraser
Smiley	Bill Owen
Len	Milo O'Shea
Battleaxe woman	Judith Furse
Molly	Renee Houston
Father with wife expecting baby	Jim Dale
Anthea	Amanda Barrie
Sarge	Cyril Chamberlain
Dancy	Peter Gilmore
District Nurse	Noel Dyson
Bridegroom	Peter Byrne

Crew list

Written by Talbot Rothwell, based on an original idea by S. C. Green and R. M. Hills

Music	Eric Rogers
Cinematography	Alan Hume BSC
Art Director	Jack Stephens
Producer	Peter Rogers
Director	Gerald Thomas

Certificate U (black and white) **Running time: approx. 91 minutes**

CARRY ON JACK

1963

'Kiss me, Hardy...'
'Are you mad, Sir? What will they say at the admiralty?'
'They'll only be jealous.'

Mutiny on the Bounty? Not quite. High sea jinks ensue as it's all aboard the good ship Venus (no, not that one!) where the quaking Captain Fearless is more concerned about the chronic gout in his right foot than in the welfare of his crew. Meanwhile Midshipman Albert Poop-Decker is not a lucky man because after winning his commission after years of struggle, his identity, rank and uniform are stolen by Sally,

Bernard Cribbins learns the *Carry On* ropes as Albert Poop-Decker.

Cast list

Captain Fearless	Kenneth Williams
Albert Poop-Decker	Bernard Cribbins
Sally	Juliet Mills
Walter Sweetley	Charles Hawtrey
First Officer Howett	Donald Houston
Angel	Percy Herbert
Carrier	Jim Dale
Patch	Peter Gilmore
Spanish governor	Patrick Cargill
First Sea Lord	Cecil Parker
Hook	Ed Devereaux
Admiral Nelson	Jimmy Thompson
Hardy	Anton Rodgers
Ancient carrier	Ian Wilson
Ned/Clown	George Woodbridge
Coach driver	John Brooking

Crew list

Written by	Talbot Rothwell
Music	Eric Rogers
Cinematography	Alan Hume BSC
Art Director	Jack Shampan
Producer	Peter Rogers
Director	Gerald Thomas

Certificate A/PG (colour) Running time: approx. 91 minutes

the girl who also stole his heart. She then proceeds to impersonate him on board whilst he ends up as one of the crew, befriended only by Walter, the press-gang victim. As mutiny ensues, Albert finds his troubles have gone from bad to worse as he's forced to walk the plank with Captain Fearless on his back.

Familiar Faces

Juliet Mills: Daughter of Sir John and sister of Hayley, Juliet was the star of many films throughout the 1960s and 1970s and still makes films today.

Donald Houston: Familiar from character parts throughout the 1950s and 1960s, he was also in the early *Doctor* films.

Cecil Parker: Character actor from such classics as *The Ladykillers* and *The Man in the White Suit*.

Captain Fearless might not live up to his name if he could see who was at the helm!

The Verdict

The first of the historical epics the team made, but by no means the best. Perhaps the presence of more of the regular stars would have made it feel more like a *Carry On* but nevertheless, there's plenty to amuse and both Williams and Hawtrey are in fine scene-stealing mode. The second film to be made in colour, full use is made of making the restricted settings seem as vivid and realistic as possible, with the costume designer really going to town on historical accuracy. The highlight has to be the scene where Williams' leg has to be amputated.

CARRY ON SPYING

1964

'Oh, hello. I just wanted to say that your father was the illegitimate son of a flea-picker's daughter!'

'Ah! You knew my father!'

The name's Bond, Ja— Well, actually, it's Simpkins, Desmond Simpkins. With three extra-special agents by his side, Simpkins' mission is to take on the malevolent powers of STENCH, namely Dr Crow, Milchmann and The Fat Man, members of the Society for the Extinction of Non-Conforming Humans. Clues as to the exact location of STENCH HQ lead the quartet of spies into the heart of Harry Lime country in Vienna, the Casbah and finally into the corridors of the Orient Express.

Familiar Faces

Richard Wattis: Fondly remembered as the interfering neighbour in *Sykes*.

John Bluthal: Later the star of *Never Mind the Quality, Feel the Width*.

The Verdict

New heights of invention and parody are reached as the *Carry On* team enter 007 territory in a joyful pastiche of the real thing with a lot more besides thrown in for good measure. There are so many scenes that work brilliantly, ranging from Dale's attempts to pass a message on to Williams, to

Cast list

Desmond Simpkins	Kenneth Williams
Harold Crump	Bernard Cribbins
Daphne Honeybutt	Barbara Windsor
James Bind	Charles Hawtrey
The Chief	Eric Barker
Carstairs	Jim Dale
Cobley	Richard Wattis
The Fat Man	Eric Pohlmann
Lila	Dilys Laye
Milchmann	Victor Maddern
Dr Crow	Judith Furse
Headwaiter	John Bluthal
Madame	Renee Houston
Doorman	Tom Clegg
Professor Stark	Frank Forsyth

Crew list

Written by	Talbot Rothwell and Sid Colin
Music	Eric Rogers
Cinematography	Alan Hume BSC
Art Director	Alex Vetchinsky
Producer	Peter Rogers
Director	Gerald Thomas

Certificate A/PG (black and white) Running time: approx. 87 minutes

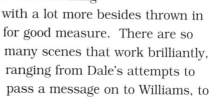

the elaborate last scene, where The Fat Man tries to dispose of Simpkins and Co. in the STENCH lair. Windsor is extremely effective and it's a pity that *Carry On Spying* is somewhat forgotten as it's a real comic gem.

"Sir, why are you talking into that Ladyshave?"

CARRY ON CLEO

1964

'So, you are the great Caesar.'
'Ah, you recognise me.'
'I have seen your bust.'
'I wish I could say the same!'

In ancient Britain the hopeful but hopeless inventor Hengist Pod comes up with his greatest device to date: a square wheel to stop carts from rolling downhill. Fate intervenes and soon both he and his neighbour, Horsa, are captured by invading Romans and sold off as slaves by the bartering brothers, Marcus and Spencius. Caesar, meanwhile, is having a bad time - he's caught flu from Britain's damp climate and is unaware that his best general, Mark Antony, has joined up with Cleopatra, Queen of Egypt, to overthrow him. When Horsa and Hengist escape from slavery by hiding in the vestal virgins' main office, they inadvertently save Caesar from an assassin's attack. As a result, the whimpering Hengist is made Caesar's champion and goes straight to the top of Mark Antony's hit list.

Familiar Faces
Sheila Hancock: Acclaimed classical actress who at the time was best known for her appearance in the sitcom *The Rag Trade*.
Warren Mitchell: On the brink of making his TV debut as the immortal Alf Garnett in *Till Death Us Do Part*, which ran for over twenty years.
Wanda Ventham: Future co-star on *UFO*.

The Verdict
Alongside *Carry On Doctor* and *Carry On up the Khyber*, this is the one people remember.

"Try it, it makes you look great. I used to be Bernard Bresslaw."

Cast list

Julius Caesar	Kenneth Williams
Mark Antony	Sid James
Hengist Pod	Kenneth Connor
Seneca	Charles Hawtrey
Calpurnia	Joan Sims
Horsa	Jim Dale
Cleopatra	Amanda Barrie
Gloria	Julie Stephens
Senna Pod	Sheila Hancock
Sergeant Major	Victor Maddern
Soothsayer	John Pertwee
Agrippa	Francis de Wolff
Archimedes	Michael Ward
Brutus	Brian Oulton
Sosages	Tom Clegg
Virginia	Tanya Binning
Bilius	David Davenport
Galley master	Peter Gilmore
Spencius	Warren Mitchell
Marcus	Gertan Klauber
Pretty bidder	Wanda Ventham
Narrator	E. V. H. Emmett

Crew list

Written by Talbot Rothwell, from an original idea by William Shakespeare

Music	Eric Rogers
Cinematography	Alan Hume BSC
Art Director	Bert Davey
Producer	Peter Rogers
Director	Gerald Thomas

Certificate A/PG (colour) Running time: approx. 92 minutes

Carry On Laughing

Quite rightly acclaimed as one of the best *Carry On*s to have been made, it stands the test of time and is still hilarious today. Everything works, from Rothwell's outrageous reworking of historical events to the impressive sets and costumes. All the performances are top notch; Williams' line of 'Infamy! Infamy! They've all got it in fer me!' has moved into cinematic legend, and his performance of Julius Caesar is the best of his whole *Carry On* repertoire. James makes Mark Antony a cockney rogue and all the other regulars perform brilliantly. Undoubtedly the best of all the historical send-ups.

"Ah, the future ...I see a police box spinning through space ..."

CARRY ON COWBOY

'They got away with forty cows.'
'Bullocks.'
'I know what I'm talking about.'

Stodge City lies in the heart of the Wild West, and the Rumpo Kid and his gang are terrorising the local community. In a desperate bid to bring his reign of fear to an end, Judge Burke sends for a sheriff and ends up getting an accident-prone sanitary engineer instead. Marshall P. Knutt has been mistaken for a gunslinger and when he's told to clean up Stodge City he thinks that means unblocking the drains. Luckily for him, help is at hand in the voluptuous shape of Annie Oakley, out to avenge her father's murderer who happens to be the Rumpo Kid.

Familiar Faces

Davey Kaye: Diminutive comedy character actor seen in dozens of British comedies.

Sydney Bromley: A British Gabby Hays, he specialised in playing the typical 'little old man' in countless films.

Richard O'Brien: Creator of *The Rocky Horror Show* and *The Crystal Maze*, he makes an appearance here as a cowboy extra!

Judge Burke has had enough of Rumpo.

The Verdict

There's a gritty, hard-edged realism behind the laughs in *Carry On Cowboy*, and it's certainly the most violent of all the films with the highest death count! Fast paced and action packed, with elaborate sets thrown in,

**Angela Douglas keeps it clean as
Annie Oakley.**

Cast list

The Rumpo Kid	Sid James
Judge Burke	Kenneth Williams
Marshall P. Knutt	Jim Dale
Big Heap	Charles Hawtrey
Belle	Joan Sims
Annie Oakley	Angela Douglas
Doc	Peter Butterworth
Little Heap	Bernard Bresslaw
Charlie	Percy Herbert
Sheriff	Jon Pertwee
Dolores	Edina Ronay
Sam	Sydney Bromley
Curly	Peter Gilmore
Josh	Davey Kaye
Commissioner Fiddler	Alan Gifford
Blacksmith	Tom Clegg
Miss Jones	Margaret Nolan
Dancing Girls	Ballet Montparnesse

Crew list

Written by	Talbot Rothwell
Music	Eric Rogers
Cinematography	Alan Hume BSC
Art Director	Bert Davey
Producer	Peter Rogers
Director	Gerald Thomas

Certificate A/PG (colour) Running time: approx. 95 minutes

it's hardly surprising that it's one of director Gerald Thomas's favourites. The cast make valiant attempts to maintain American accents, with the most convincing belonging to - surprisingly - Sid James, who made no attempt to disguise his accent in any other film, either before or after this one. Rothwell's script is extremely inventive, sending up a genre that he clearly knows back to front, while the end result has an ambitious quality to it that is quite striking. Definitely ranks in the top five!

CARRY ON SCREAMING

'We can't afford to leave any stone unturned. What's the name of this road, Slobotham?'
'Er ... Avery Avenue, Sir.'
'Well, like I said. We must explore Avery Avenue!'

Familiar Faces

Harry H. Corbett: Forever remembered as Albert Steptoe from the long-running *Steptoe and Son*.

Frank Thornton: Remembered as Captain

During an amorous evening in the woods with his girlfriend, Albert is forced to go to the police station after his beloved Doris goes missing - all that's left in her place is a severed hairy finger which Albert quickly realises is not hers. Detective Sergeant Bung and his assistant, Slobotham, are right on the case and are soon knocking on the door of the mysterious Doctor Watt and his ravishing sister Valaria. Bung is soon under her spell and it's up to Albert to try and draw him back to the case when it becomes all too obvious that Doctor Watt is kidnapping young women, immersing them in wax and turning them into shop window dummies. Alongside Bung, Albert has to face the monstrous Oddbod and Oddbod Junior, and it's then they discover Doctor Watt's potion for turning people into werewolves...

Cast list

Character	Actor
Detective Sergeant Bung	Harry H. Corbett
Doctor Watt	Kenneth Williams
Albert	Jim Dale
Valaria	Fenella Fielding
Emily Bung	Joan Sims
Dan Dan	Charles Hawtrey
Detective Constable Slobotham	Peter Butterworth
Sockett	Bernard Bresslaw
Doris Mann	Angela Douglas
Doctor Fettle	Jon Pertwee
Oddbod	Tom Clegg
Oddbod Junior	Billy Cornelius
Mr Jones	Frank Thornton
Vivian	Michael Ward
Cabby	Norman Mitchell
Desk Sergeant	Frank Forsyth
Policeman	Anthony Sagar

Crew list

Written by	Talbot Rothwell
Music	Eric Rogers
Cinematography	Alan Hume BSC
Art Director	Bert Davey
Producer	Peter Rogers
Director	Gerald Thomas

Certificate A/PG (colour) Running time: approx. 97 minutes

Peacock in the 70s sitcom, *Are You Being Served?*

Joan Sims gives a rather rigid performance when Emily Bung comes to grief.

The Verdict

Following the success of *Carry On Cowboy*, the *Carry On* team leapt for the jugular by taking on the horror genre, then enjoying a massive revival courtesy of the legendary Hammer Horror films. *Carry On Screaming* is probably one of the most consistently funny of the *Carry On* films, with Rothwell's sparkling script ranking alongside *Cleo* and

Khyber for laughs. The performances are all spot on, with Williams and Fielding making a marvellously camp double act. Dale and Butterworth are also wonderful comic foils, with Dale's finest hour coming when he sprouts fangs and facial hair! Great fun all round.

CARRY ON - DON'T LOSE YOUR HEAD!

'Psst!'
'What?'
'Psst!'
'Don't be ridiculous - I've only had a couple!'

Move out of the way, Scarlet Pimpernel, the Black Fingernail is here! France is awash with the blood of the aristocracy at the height of the Revolution and it's up to Sir Rodney Ffing, normally a member of the idle rich, and his fellow effete slob, Lord Darcy, to rescue the Duc de Pommfrit from the guillotine. In reality the unremarkable Rodney Ffing is really the Black Fingernail, master of disguise and enemy of Citizen Camembert, the Terror of Paris.

Familiar Faces

Dany Robin: French leading actress who branched into English language films early on in her career.

Jacqueline Pearce: Later achieved cult status as the villainess in BBC's *Blake's Seven*.

Julian Orchard: Popular character actor, often seen in comedy films but has also made a couple of more 'serious' appearances.

Citizen Camembert, supported by Citizen Bidet.

Lord Darcy in disguise with the Duc de Pommfrit and Sir Rodney Ffing.

Cast list

Sir Rodney Ffing	Sid James
Citizen Camembert	Kenneth Williams
Lord Darcy	Jim Dale
Duc de Pommfrit	Charles Hawtrey
Citizen Bidet	Peter Butterworth
Desiree DuBarry	Joan Sims
Jacqueline	Dany Robin
Robespierre	Peter Gilmore
Landlady	Marianne Stone
Henri	Michael Ward
Malabonce the executioner	Leon Greene
Sergeant	David Davenport
Rake	Julian Orchard
First lady	Jennifer Clulow
Second lady	Valerie van Ost
Third lady	Jacqueline Pearce
Soldier	Billy Cornelius

Crew list

Written by	Talbot Rothwell
Music	Eric Rogers
Cinematography	Terry Gilbert
Art Director	Lionel Couch
Producer	Peter Rogers
Director	Gerald Thomas

Certificate A/PG (colour) Running time: approx. 90 minutes

The Verdict

The most elaborate of the historical *Carry Ons*, ranking second to *Cleo* in terms of effort to realise historical accuracy - at least in terms of visual presentation. James is at his most athletic, sword-fighting best with Dale proving to be an equally adept sparring partner. It's clear they revel in the chance to play around in the character disguises they don, but James looks remarkably ill at ease when dressed up as an old hag. Williams and Hawtrey are as reliable as ever, while Butterworth continues to display his increasing habit of stealing scenes when he's in them. Rothwell's script does tend to struggle under the weight of knowledge that exists about the Revolution but nevertheless, it's great fun and well worth a look.

CARRY ON - FOLLOW THAT CAMEL

1967

'Hold it, baby. How about giving us the Dance of the Two Veils.'
'You mean Seven Veils.'
'Why bother with preliminaries!'

After being accused of ungentlemanly behaviour during a cricket match, Bertram Oliphant West does what any self-respecting gentleman would do, and giving up the hand of his fiancée takes off, with grumbling butler Simpson in tow, to join the Foreign Legion. The fort he ends up in is run by the roguish Sergeant Knocker but this doesn't stop Lady Jane Ponsonby, Bo West's ex-fiancée, from trying to find him. In amongst all this confusion the fort comes under siege from Sheikh Abdul Abulbul, whose battle cry is in the name of his prophet, Mustapha Leek!

Familiar Faces
Anita Harris: Singer and entertainer who found fame in the late 1960s.
William Mervyn: Fondly remembered as the retired detective *Mr Rose*.
Julian Holloway: Son of Stanley Holloway who became a *Carry On* regular.

Phil Silvers celebrated his birthday making *Follow That Camel*.

The Verdict
Camel is basically Sergeant Bilko in the desert, with Phil Silvers giving the same performance as his character is Bilko rehashed. Rothwell took full advantage and

Carry On Laughing

worked in all the tricks and dynamics that the Bilko writers had developed with Silvers, and they work perfectly although Silvers does seem on edge for most of the film. There seems to be a running battle going on between Silvers and Williams in who can overact the most, and it's Williams who wins with his outrageous cod-French/German accent. Dale and Butterworth make a fine Laurel and Hardy-like team, with many of the gags that the

Cast list

Sergeant Knocker	Phil Silvers
Commandant Burger	Kenneth Williams
Bertram Oliphant West	Jim Dale
Captain Le Pice	Charles Hawtrey
Simpson	Peter Butterworth
Zigzig	Joan Sims
Sheikh Abdul Abulbul	Bernard Bresslaw
Lady Jane Ponsonby	Angela Douglas
Corktip	Anita Harris
Corporal Clotski	John Bluthal
Sir Cyril Ponsonby	William Mervyn
Captain Bagshaw	Peter Gilmore
Ticket collector	Julian Holloway
Riff	Larry Taylor
Raff	William Hurndall
Doctor	Julian Orchard
Hotel manager in Algiers	David Glover
Ship's officer	Vincent Ball

Crew list

Written by	Talbot Rothwell
Music	Eric Rogers
Cinematography	Alan Hume BSc
Art Director	Alex Vetchinsky
Producer	Peter Rogers
Director	Gerald Thomas

Certificate A/PG (colour) Running time: approx. 90 minutes

Sergeant Knocker inspects some of his namesakes.

classic duo had performed in their Foreign Legion films being repeated here. Both Bresslaw and Hawtrey are obviously enjoying their roles. Visually impressive desert scenes make the whole thing seem more spectacular than it actually is. *Follow That Camel* was not originally intended as a *Carry On* but was retitled several years later, as obviously it can't be anything else but one!

CARRY ON DOCTOR

1967

'Young chickens may be soft and tender but the older birds have more on them.'
'True. And take a lot more stuffing!'

- or -
Nurse Carries On Again
- or -
Death of a Daffodil
- or -
Life is a Four-Lettered Word

After an accident mid-sermon, faith healer Francis Bigger finds himself immersed in the hijinks of hospital life, where the effusive Doctor Kilmore is the most popular doctor on the wards, among both nurses and patients. After getting involved in a tangle with nurse Sandra May on a rooftop, where he mistakes her sunbathing repose for a suicide bid, the officious and arrogant Doctor Tinkle joins forces with the formidable matron to get rid of him. There is a problem, however, as they have not taken the patients into consideration or the lengths they will go to to get the good doctor reinstated.

Familiar Faces

Derek Francis: Comedy character actor, long associated with sitcoms where he invariably played a vicar or company boss.

Dandy Nichols: Spent the best part of a decade playing the long-suffering Elsie, wife of *Till Death Us Do Part*'s Alf Garnett.

Peter Jones: Comedy actor familiar on screen from *The Rag Trade* but he will be remembered on radio as the voice of *The Hitch Hiker's Guide to the Galaxy*.

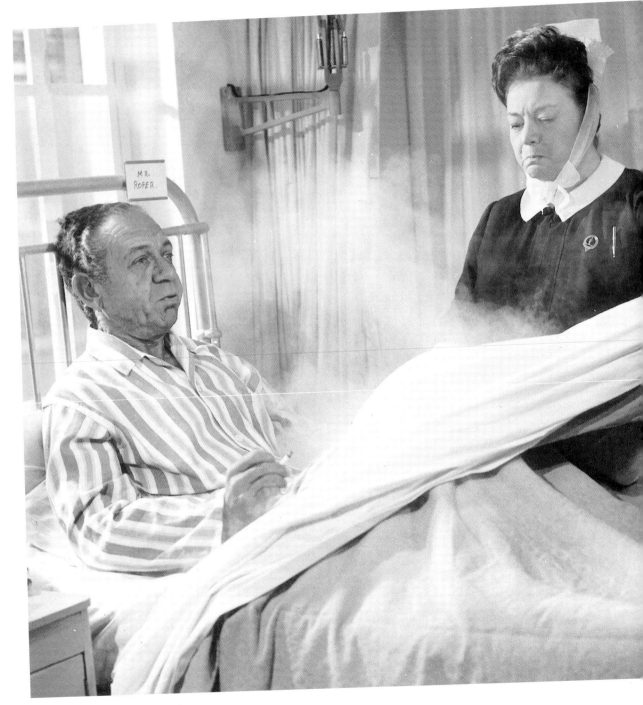

Matron exposes Charlie Roper's butt.

Deryck Guyler: Player of washboards and Corky the Policeman in *Sykes*, which ran for the best part of two decades on BBC.

Brian Wilde: Now familiar as Foggy in *Last of the Summer Wine*.

Pat Coombs: Comedy actress, long-time stooge to the larger-than-life Peggy Mount. Most recently a cast member in *EastEnders*.

Penelope Keith: Star of countless sitcoms, but most memorable in *The Good Life*.

The Verdict

A close second to *Carry On Nurse* as the best of the medical mayhem movies. The fact that all of the regular team are present makes this one more than a little memorable, and the banter between Jacques and Williams works so well that it's clear why they tried it again in both *Carry On Again Doctor* and *Carry On Matron*. Very much an ensemble piece for the cast playing the patients; even though Howerd is the big 'guest star', he's soon relegated to being part of the patient gang. There's one surrealistic piece with an invisible patient which jars slightly, but other than that it's a welcome respite from the onslaught of historical epics the team was making, and is certainly one of the better *Carry Ons*.

Cast list

Francis Bigger	Frankie Howerd
Charlie Roper	Sid James
Doctor Tinkle	Kenneth Williams
Doctor Kilmore	Jim Dale
Mr Barron	Charles Hawtrey
Matron	Hattie Jacques
Nurse Sandra May	Barbara Windsor
Chloe Gibson	Joan Sims
Ken Biddle	Bernard Bresslaw
Mr Smith	Peter Butterworth
Nurse Clarke	Anita Harris
Sister Hoggett	June Jago
Sir Edmund Burke	Derek Francis
Mrs Roper	Dandy Nichols
Chaplain	Peter Jones
Surgeon Hardcastle	Deryck Guyler
Mrs Barron	Gwendolyn Watts
Mavis	Dilys Lane
Henry	Peter Gilmore
Sam	Harry Locke
Nurse Parkin	Valerie van Ost
Mrs Smith	Jean St Clair
Fred	Julian Orchard
Man from Cox & Carter	Brian Wilde
Patient	Pat Coombs
Simmons	Julian Holloway
Night porter	Gordon Rollings
Plain nurse	Penelope Keith

Crew list

Written by	Talbot Rothwell
Music	Eric Rogers
Cinematography	Alan Hume BSc
Art Director	Cedric Dawe
Producer	Peter Rogers
Director	Gerald Thomas

Certificate A/PG (colour) **Running time: approx. 94 minutes**

CARRY ON UP THE KHYBER

'Oh I say! The wind seems a little strong tonight.'
'Whose?'

- or -
The British Position in India

When *the* **Khasi** of Kalabar gets his hands on some information that proves beyond doubt that the men of the Third Foot and Mouth Regiment are not the 'Devils in Skirts' of repute, he decides to bring their presence in India to a bloody end. Sir Sidney Ruff-Diamond, the epitome of English stiff upper

Brother Belcher, Private Widdle and Lady Ruff Diamond fail to impress as dancing girls from the Khasi's harem.

Captain Keene gives Princess Jelhi a lift.

lipness, tries to bring the Khasi's plans to a peaceful end but when he realises his actions could bring about the end of his cushy job, his resolve weakens. He is further hampered by the behaviour of his good lady wife, who has the proverbial hots for the Khasi.

Familiar Faces
Roy Castle: The late lamented entertainer who presented *Record Breakers* for the BBC and dabbled in an occasional bit of acting, made his one and only *Carry On* appearance here.
Johnny Briggs: Now better known as *Coronation Street*'s Mike Baldwin.

The Verdict
The best. Quite simply the height of achievement on all fronts, from Rothwell's sparkling script through to extensive location work and the performances which all hit the right spot. This is the *Carry On* to introduce novices to the series with. If this one doesn't convert them, check they've got a pulse. All the actors are clearly having a ball on screen. James is at his most deadpan while Williams goes for broke with nostrils in full-flare mode for most of the film. At the time people speculated that this one would be impossible to top and the series would go into decline soon after. Certainly *Carry On Up the Khyber* was never topped, but as for decline ... there was life in the old dog yet!

CARRY ON AGAIN DOCTOR

1969

'Marvellous! Rain for nine months, hurricanes for three!' 'Yes, that's why the natives call these islands "Orlpice Na Fa-Fah"... it's all rain and wind!'

Doctor Nookey falls head over heels in love with one of his patients, an actress by the name of Goldie Locks. During his date with her at the hospital's Christmas party, he unknowingly drinks a spiced-up punch and causes chaos in the wards. Rather than sack him, Doctor Carver uses him as a pawn in his plan to gain money for the Frederick Carver Foundation, and sends him on a medical mission to the remote Beatific Islands. There, Nookey finds Gladstone Screwer in residence, who has discovered the formula for a slimming potion. Back in England, Nookey makes his fortune from it but Carver won't rest until he has the ingredients in his possession.

Dr Nookey injects Lady Puddleton (a disguised Dr Stoppidge) with a slimming potion of gnat's milk, banyan tree juice and powdered parrot droppings.

- or -
Where There's a Pill
There's a Way
- or -
The Bowels are
rInging
- or -
If You Say It's Your
Thermometer I'll Have
to Believe You but it's
a Funny
Place to Put It!

The entire end sequence seems as if it suffered heavily in editing, with the climax suddenly cutting to an oddly happy ending with all the main characters getting married in one mass ceremony. It's entertaining, but by no means one of the best.

Dr Nookey deep in discussion with Dr Carver.

Familiar Faces

Wilfred Bramble: Steptoe senior in the long-running *Steptoe and Son*. He had a wordless cameo appearance.

Patricia Hayes: Acclaimed actress who was one of Tony Hancock's regular accomplices.

Shakira Baksh: Not the most familiar of names but in 1967 she had been Miss Guyana and would go on to become Mrs Michael Caine.

Bob Todd: Moon-faced comedy actor who was a long-term stooge to Benny Hill.

The Verdict

The least successful of the medical *Carry Ons*, with a plot that seems to be settling down as a hospital-based frolic when suddenly it veers off wildly to a tropical island, bringing in Sid James at a late stage. Some of the gags are a bit laboured and the whole film is a bit of a mess. Williams and Hawtrey continue their tradition of working as a double act in many scenes, playing to each other perfectly, while James is strangely wasted by not being given enough to do.

Cast list

Gladstone Screwer	Sid James
Doctor Frederick Carver	Kenneth Williams
Doctor Ernest Stoppidge	Charles Hawtrey
Doctor James Nookey	Jim Dale
Goldie Locks	Barbara Windsor
Matron	Hattie Jacques
Mrs Ellen Moore	Joan Sims
Miss Fosdick	Patsy Rowlands
Mr Pullen	Wilfred Bramble
Male patient	Peter Butterworth
Nurse Willing	Elizabeth Knight
Henry	Peter Gilmore
Miss Armitage	Pat Coombs
Mrs Beasley	Patricia Hayes
Lord Paragon	William Mervyn
Stout woman	Alexandra Dane
Porter	Harry Locke
Deirdre	Valerie Leon
Old lady with headphones	Lucy Griffiths
Night sister	Gwendolyn Watts
Out-patients sister	Valerie van Ost
Patient in plaster	Billy Cornelius
Scrubba	Shakira Baksh
Mr Bean	Frank Forsyth
Patient	Bob Todd

Crew list

Written by	Talbot Rothwell
Music	Eric Rogers
Cinematography	Ernest Steward BSc
Art Director	John Blezard
Producer	Peter Rogers
Director	Gerald Thomas

Certificate A/PG (colour) Running time: approx. 89 minutes

Carry On Camping

- or -
Let Sleeping Bags Lie

'What's a nice girl like you doing with an old cow?'
'I'm taking her to the bull.'
'To the bull! Couldn't your father do that!'
'No. It has to be the bull.'

Sid Boggle is determined to drag his best friend, Bernie Lugg, and their respective girlfriends, Joan and Anthea, off on a holiday they'll never forget ... to a naturist camp! On arrival, however, they find it's just a normal campsite. Things pick up for Sid and Bernie with the arrival of Doctor Soaper, Miss Haggard and their pupils, a gaggle of man-hungry teenage girls who camp down next to them. Elsewhere on the campsite, weary businessman Peter Potter is carefully planning how to dispose of irritating backpacker Charlie Muggins, who has grafted himself on to Peter's holiday.

Familiar Faces
Valerie Leon: Hammer starlet of the highest order who is also remembered for her infamous 'Hi Karate' ads in the mid-1970s.
Anna Karen: Went on to become the long-suffering wife of Michael Robins in the sitcom *On the Buses*.

The Verdict
Second only in quality to *Carry On Up the Khyber*, this is probably one of the most famous films in the series and that's in no small part due to the first flash of exposed female flesh to have graced the screen under the *Carry On* banner. The flesh belonged to Barbara Windsor, taking part in a workout clad in only a small bikini. Williams and Jacques are on top form, continuing with the same kind of repartee they enjoyed in *Carry On Doctor*. In fact, the merest hint is dropped in one scene that Jacques' character is actually that same matron; something which is implied in all the medical *Carry On*s in what has to

Cast list

Sid Boggle	Sid James
Doctor Soaper	Kenneth Williams
Charlie Muggins	Charles Hawtrey
Joan Fussey	Joan Sims
Peter Potter	Terry Scott
Miss Haggard	Hattie Jacques
Bernie Lugg	Bernard Bresslaw
Babs	Barbara Windsor
Jim Tanner	Julian Holloway
Anthea Meeks	Dilys Laye
Joshua Fiddler	Peter Butterworth
Harriet Potter	Betty Marsden
Sally	Trisha Noble
Mrs Fussey	Amelia Bayntun
Store manager	Brian Oulton
Farmer's daughter	Patricia Franklin
Farmer	Derek Francis
Hefty girl	Anna Karen
Store assistant	Valerie Leon

Crew list

Written by	Talbot Rothwell
Music	Eric Rogers
Cinematography	Ernest Steward BSc
Art Director	Lionel Couch
Producer	Peter Rogers
Director	Gerald Thomas

Certificate A/PG (colour) Running time: approx. 88 minutes

Peter Potter pours a pot of paltry pap on poor pathetic Charlie.

be the most extraordinary piece of continuity in cinema history! James and Bresslaw make a good team, but the show stealers are, as ever, Williams and Jacques, and in this case Terry Scott as well. Next to

Carry On Up the Khyber, this is the one to induct the novice with.

167

CARRY ON UP THE JUNGLE

1969

An expedition winds its perilous way through the jungles of darkest Africa. Different members of this party have all had different reasons for making the trek: Professor Inigo Tinkle is an ornithologist searching for the extremely rare Oozlum Bird which has a habit of disappearing up its own ... well, you know; Lady Evelyn Bagley is on a quest to find her long lost son who went missing in the jungle

> - or -
> *The African Queen*
> - or -
> *Stop Beating About the Bush*
> - or -
> *Show Me Your Waterhole and I'll Show You Mine*

as a baby; and Bill Boosey, trapper and hunter of notorious repute, has come along for the adventure. Along the way they find a jungle boy who could possibly be Lady Bagley's son, but a more disturbing discovery is made when Lady Bagley finds that her husband, who went missing with the boy, is now the King of Lovers to a tribe of 4000 love-hungry women.

Familiar Faces
Nina Baden-Semper: Went on to play the wife of Rudolph Walker in the very politically incorrect sitcom from the 1970s, *Love Thy Neighbour*.

The Verdict
Nice idea, shame about the execution. In trying to set something in such an exotic location, the whole thing hits an immediate brick wall because there was no way that the notorious tight purse strings of a *Carry On* budget could have stretched to take cast and crew to a real jungle. What we get instead is

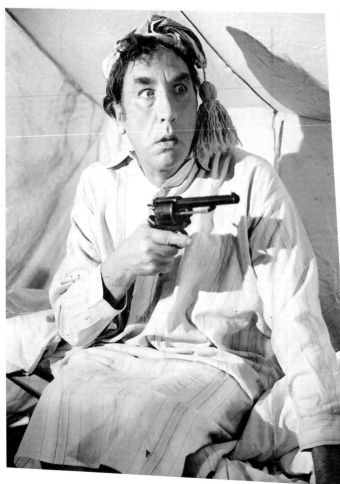

Professor Inigo Tinkle covers his opening.

Cast list

Professor Inigo Tinkle	Frankie Howerd
Bill Boosey	Sid James
Lady Evelyn Bagley	Joan Sims
Claude Chumley	Kenneth Connor
Tonka	Charles Hawtrey
Jungle boy	Terry Scott
Upsidasi	Bernard Bresslaw
June	Jacki Piper
Leda	Valerie Leon
Nerda	Edwina Carroll
Lubi Lieutenant	Valerie Moore
Nosha	Nina Baden-Semper
Gorilla	Reuben Martin

Crew list

Written by	Talbot Rothwell
Music	Eric Rogers
Cinematography	Ernest Steward BSc
Art Director	Alex Vetchinsky
Producer	Peter Rogers
Director	Gerald Thomas

Certificate A/PG (colour) Running time: approx. 89 minutes

a painfully obvious studio set with the inevitable stock footage of various wild animals plus an actor dressed up in a gorilla outfit. There are, however, pearls to be found amongst the mire; Howerd is good value and so is Sims in the scene where she thinks a man is making improper advances towards her at the dinner table when in fact it's a snake winding up her leg. The film is at best only an average *Carry On*. Williams is sorely missed.

The intrepid explorers are led into the jungle by Upsidasi.

A Celebration

CARRY ON LOVING

1970

'The first wife died from eating mushrooms.'
'Oh, I'm sorry to hear that.'
'So was she. The second wife died from a fractured skull.'
'Fractured skull? How did that happen?'
'She wouldn't eat the mushrooms.'

Sidney and Sophie Bliss constantly hurl insults at each other, but as soon as someone crosses the threshold of their Wedded Bliss computer dating agency, they quickly put on a show of loving devotion. They are the ultimate advert for their own company and various inhabitants of Much-Snogging-in-the-Green seek their assistance in finding the perfect mate. Terence Philpot's initial impression of the seemingly plain Jenny Grubb soon

Cast list

Sidney Bliss	Sid James
Percival Snooper	Kenneth Williams
James Bedsop	Charles Hawtrey
Esme Crowfoot	Joan Sims
Sophie Bliss	Hattie Jacques
Terence Philpot	Terry Scott
Gripper Burke	Bernard Bresslaw
Bertie Muffet	Richard O'Callaghan
Sally Martin	Jacki Piper
Jenny Grubb	Imogen Hassall
Adrian	Julian Holloway
Mrs Grubb	Joan Hickson
Miss Dempsey	Patsy Rowlands
Aunt Victoria Grubb	Ann Way
Mr Dreery	Bill Maynard
Trainer	Tom Clegg
Woman	Lucy Griffiths
Man in hospital	Anthony Sagar
Bishop	Derek Francis
Emily	Alexandra Dane
Wife	Anna Karen
Husband	Lauri Lupino Lane
Barman	Bill Pertwee
Bus conductor	Kenny Lynch
Mr Thrush	Norman Chappell
Mr Roxby	James Beck
Mrs Roxby	Yutte Stensgaard
Marriage bureau client	Peter Butterworth

Crew list

Written by	Talbot Rothwell
Music	Eric Rogers
Cinematography	Ernest Steward BSc
Art Director	Lionel Couch
Producer	Peter Rogers
Director	Gerald Thomas

Certificate A/PG (colour) Running time: approx. 88 minutes

changes when she breaks free from her domineering parents, the simpering Bertie Muffet falls for Sally Martin, while Sid is dating Esme Crowfoot behind Sophie's back. Sophie is determined to make him jealous and win him back, so she

Terry Scott registers surprise but...

puts to good use the tools at her disposal.

...the master shows how it's really done.

Familiar Faces

Bill Maynard: Character actor who played Selwyn Froggett, but these days appears in *Heartbeat*.

Bill Pertwee: Cousin of Jon, best remembered as the grumbling air raid warden in *Dad's Army*.

Kenny Lynch: Singer and entertainer from the 1960s onwards.

James Beck: Another *Dad's Army* regular, easily identified as the one who played the 'spiv'.

The Verdict

A 'back to basics' sort of *Carry On*, reminiscent of the early films. There's no strong backbone to the plot but a collection of sketches bound together by James and Jacques in the Sid and Sophie Bliss roles. It appears that Rothwell seems to have become lost towards the end of the script in trying to figure out a finale, so he pulls the oldest trick out of the book and brings the entire cast together in a pie fight. There are, however, lots of naughty and coy sex scenes, and sex sells at the cinema. The result was that *Carry On Loving* was enormous at the box-office even though the film itself is enjoyably about average.

A Celebration

CARRY ON HENRY

- or -
Mind My Chopper
- or - (and this one was cut
from the titles before the film's release!)
Anne of a Thousand Lays

1970

'A drink, Ma'am?'
'Thank you.'
'I can heartily recommend the porter here.'
'Really? Then do send him up to my room later.'

The adult life and many, many loves of King Henry VIII are chronicled here by one William Cobbler, so the work can quite rightly be

described as Cobbler's. With one wife freshly beheaded, King Henry is at the alter with Queen Marie. Cardinal Wolsey is conducting the wedding service but Henry just wants him to hurry up as he's eager to get to the bed chamber. Sadly, once there, he discovers his new wife stinks of garlic so he wants a divorce. As Marie is sister to the king of France, this is not easy, but then Henry's eyes alight on the lovely Bettina, daughter of the Earl of Bristol. He has to have her - and her dowry - at all costs, so plots to get rid of his French queen.

Familiar Faces

Dave Prowse: More famous as the man behind the Darth Vader mask in all three *Star Wars* films and also the Green Cross Code Man.

David Essex: Yes, that David Essex! Before his singing career took off he had half a day's work on this *Carry On* as a page boy, but his performance sadly ended up on the cutting room floor during the editing stage of the movie.

Cardinal Wolsey attends the king on the throne.

Lord Hampton of Wick.

The Verdict

One of the best historical romps, ranking up there with *Cleo* and *Don't Lose Your Head*. The jokes are consistently funny and James has a ball as Henry, obviously relishing every minute. The location filming and the sets make the whole thing look ten times more expensive than it actually was and Roger's music is masterful. Although by the early 70s the films were beginning to miss their mark, *Henry* proves that the team were still capable of producing a classic, and this remains a 'must see' on the uninitiated's list.

Cast list

King Henry VIII	Sid James
Thomas Cromwell	Kenneth Williams
Sir Roger de Lodgerley	Charles Hawtrey
Queen Marie	Joan Sims
Cardinal Wolsey	Terry Scott
Bettina	Barbara Windsor
Lord Hampton of Wick	Kenneth Connor
Sir Thomas	Julian Holloway
Francis, King of France	Peter Gilmore
Duc de Poncenay	Julian Orchard
Bidet	Gertan Klauber
Major Domo	David Davenport
Buxom woman	Margaret Nolan
Physician	William Mervyn
Farmer	Derek Francis
Guy Fawkes	Bill Maynard
Warder	Dave Prowse
Queen	Patsy Rowlands
Guard	Billy Cornelius
Royal tailor	John Bluthal
Heckler	Anthony Sagar
Warder	Brian Wilde
The Earl of Bristol	Peter Butterworth

Crew list

Written by	Talbot Rothwell
Music	Eric Rogers
Cinematography	Alan Hume BSc
Art Director	Lionel Couch
Producer	Peter Rogers
Director	Gerald Thomas

Certificate A/PG (colour) **Running time: approx. 89 minutes**

A Celebration

CARRY ON AT YOUR CONVENIENCE

1971

'I can assure you, Sir, that an elephant could safely use that toilet!'
'Not without a much bigger bowl.'

- or -
Down the Spout
- or -
Ladies Please be Seated
- or -
Up the Workers
- or -
Labour Relations are the People who Come to See You When You're Having a Baby

The strike-plagued toilet manufacturers W. C. Boggs & Son are quite literally on the brink of going down the pan due to the fact that the union representative, Vic Spanner, jumps on every possible excuse that crops up to call his fellow workers out on strike. When the

Cast list

Sid Plummer	Sid James
W. C. Boggs	Kenneth Williams
Charlie Coote	Charles Hawtrey
Beattie Plummer	Hattie Jacques
Chloe Moore	Joan Sims
Bernie Hulke	Bernard Bresslaw
Vic Spanner	Kenneth Cope
Miss Withering	Patsy Rowlands
Myrtle Plummer	Jacki Piper
Lewis Boggs	Richard O'Callaghan
Fred Moore	Bill Maynard
Benny	Davy Kaye
Agatha Spanner	Renee Houston
Maud	Marianne Stone
Popsy	Margaret Nolan
Willie	Geoffrey Hughes
Ernie	Hugh Futcher
Roadhouse manager	Bill Pertwee

Crew list

Written by	Talbot Rothwell
Music	Eric Rogers
Cinematography	Ernest Steward BSc
Art Director	Lionel Couch
Producer	Peter Rogers
Director	Gerald Thomas

Certificate A/PG (colour) Running time: approx. 90 minutes

company chairman, Mr Boggs, tells factory foreman Sid Plummer that the cash has dried up, Plummer proposes an office outing to boost the workers' morale. As the factory outing gets underway, Boggs and all the other high-ranking staff members decide to join in and that's when the chaos begins.

Familiar Faces

Kenneth Cope: In the 1960s he was Jed Stone in *Coronation Street* and the dearly departed partner in *Randall and Hopkirk (Deceased)*. He went on to become a reliable supporting actor in *Doctor Who* and *Casualty*.

Renee Houston: Formidable character actress who appeared in many series during the 1960s and 1970s, usually as the domineering housewife.

Geoffrey Hughes: Remembered now as Eddie Yates from *Coronation Street* but now regularly appears in the sitcom *Keeping Up Appearances*.

The Verdict

A huge flop compared to the last few films, but that was mainly due to the sensitive subject matter; a large percentage of the *Carry On* audiences consisted of the workers they were sending up in *Convenience*. Rothwell seems to have had only a basic understanding of how the trade unions work so the end result is rather patronising and cringeworthy. This doesn't have a strong plot to save the day but many of the performances make up for the weak structuring: Jacques is wonderful as the budgie-besotted wife of James, who puts in his famous guffaw at every given opportunity. Williams is surprisingly restrained and aloof but lets rip in the Brighton scenes. *Carry On at Your Convenience* is nowhere near the kind of quality that the *Carry On* team were producing at around this time and it does unfortunately signal the beginning of a downward spiral.

A Spanner in the works blocks Boggs.

CARRY ON MATRON

1971

'But how do we know we're physically suited to each other? I mean, it's like do-it-yourself with wallpaper, isn't it?'
'Wallpaper?'
'Yes. You don't just go into a shop and buy enough for the whole room. You tear yourself off a little strip and try it first.'
'That may be so, but you're not going to stick me up against a wall!'

At the Finisham Maternity Hospital, Sir Bernard Cutting is seemingly the personification of professionalism to all who see him in the wards, but behind the locked door of his office he's convinced that he's ill. He seeks the advice of Dr Goode, who tells him he has to assert his manhood to regain his morale. Looking around the hospital, Sir Bernard's eyes fasten on the unsuspecting matron, who would far rather be watching a medical soap opera on the television!

Familiar Faces

Wendy Richard: Now a household name as Pauline in *EastEnders*, but back in the 1970s was better known as Miss Brahms in *Are You Being Served?*
Bill Kenwright: Former star of

Dr Zhivago, alias Sid Carter, alias Sid James.

- or -
From Here to Maternity
- or -
Womb at the Top
- or -
Familiarity Breeds
- or -
The Pregger's Opera

Coronation Street and now a West End impresario.
Juliet Harmer: The former sidekick of Gerald Harper in *Adam Adamant Lives* in the 1960s.

The Verdict

Better than *Carry On Again Doctor* and the

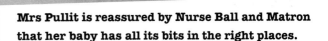

Cast list

Sid Carter	Sid James
Sir Bernard Cutting	Kenneth Williams
Dr Francis Goode	Charles Hawtrey
Matron	Hattie Jacques
Mrs Tidey	Joan Sims
Ernie	Bernard Bresslaw
Dr Prodd	Terry Scott
Nurse Susan Ball	Barbara Windsor
Mr Tidey	Kenneth Connor
Cyril Carter	Kenneth Cope
Freddy	Bill Maynard
Evelyn Banks	Patsy Rowlands
Sister	Jacki Piper
Arthur	Derek Francis
Mrs Jenkins	Amelia Bayntun
Jane Darling	Valerie Leon
Ambulance driver	Brian Osborne
Frances Kemp	Gwendoline Watts
Miss Smethurst	Valerie Shute
Mrs Tucker	Margaret Nolan
Miss Willing	Wendy Richard
Reporter	Bill Kenwright
Expectant father	Jack Douglas
Mrs Pullitt	Madeline Smith
Mrs Putzova	Marianne Stone
Mrs Bentley	Juliet Harmer

Crew list

Written by	Talbot Rothwell
Music	Eric Rogers
Cinematography	Ernest Steward BSc
Art Director	Lionel Couch
Producer	Peter Rogers
Director	Gerald Thomas

Certificate A/PG (colour) **Running time: approx. 87 minutes**

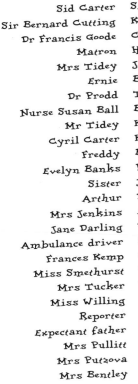

Mrs Pullit is reassured by Nurse Ball and Matron that her baby has all its bits in the right places.

last of the medical *Carry On*s to date. The film sees the main cast give some of their most outrageous performances, making the film all the better for it; Williams' performance of a man believing he is changing sex has to be seen to be believed. James is his usual rogue-like self and the sequences where he is disguised as a specialist called Doctor Zhivago are a true comic *tour-de-force*, as is Bresslaw's drag act as a pregnant woman. This, together with *Carry On Abroad*, is the last of the truly entertaining films in the series and it's noticeable that the level of raunch that becomes such a part of the later films is starting to creep in here. *Carry On Matron* is one of the best *Carry On*s of the 1970s.

CARRY ON ABROAD

'Don't you understand? I don't want just a quick roll in the hay. I need something that's going to last.'

'Who says it's not going to last? We don't go home until tomorrow afternoon!'

Stuart Farquhar is in charge of a group of tourists travelling by coach to the Spanish holiday resort of Elsbels, but on arrival they find that the hotel is far from being finished; in fact, there's no roof and no running hot and cold water. The tourists first cause chaos in the local market and end up in prison as a result, but things go from bad to worse. The final night at the hotel turns into a lustful riot when the punch is laced with Liquora Amorosa, and due to the effect this has on various couples, no one notices when the hotel floor starts to cave in!

Familiar Faces
Jimmy Logan: Popular Scottish comedian and occasional actor who briefly appeared in *Carry On Girls*.

Sally Geeson: Sister of Judy and then a regular in Sid James's sitcom *Bless This House*

Carol Hawkins: Familiar face in the classroom of 5C in *Please Sir!* and *The Fenn Street Gang*.

Ray Brooks: Popular leading man in British films of the 1960s, such as *The Knack*, and later the star of various comedy-dramas on TV, such as *Big Deal* and *Growing Pains*.

- or -
What a Package
- or -
It's All In
- or -
Swiss Hols in the Snow

Stan and Evelyn Blunt squeeze their luggage into the Elsbels bus.

The Verdict
Slightly patchy but the last truly entertaining *Carry On*, this was also the last time that such a large number of the regular cast members would be seen together, with Hawtrey's subsequent absence being very much noticed. Butterworth and Jacques steal the show as the incompetent hotel owners, whose violent arguments have a strange Laurel and Hardy feel to them. Whitfield makes quite an impact as Connor's frigid and highly opinionated wife while Logan is great as the lustful Scotsman pursuing Windsor, who is as reliable as ever. All the others are on usual top form apart

from Hawtrey, who seems to be running on automatic pilot through most of the film. Notorious for being the Carry *On* where Windsor displays more than just her acting talents in the shower scene, it's also a little sad as in a way it marks the end of an era.

Scott was gone for good, Hawtrey was now leaving and James was soon to follow.

Cast list

Vic Flange	Sid James
Stuart Farquhar	Kenneth Williams
Eustance Tuttle	Charles Hawtrey
Cora Flange	Joan Sims
Brother Bernard	Bernard Bresslaw
Sadie Tompkins	Barbara Windsor
Stanley Blunt	Kenneth Connor
Evelyn Blunt	June Whitfield
Pepe	Peter Butterworth
Floella	Hattie Jacques
Bert Conway	Jimmy Logan
Lily	Sally Geeson
Marge	Carol Hawkins
Georgio	Ray Brooks
Brother Martin	Derek Francis
Robin	John Clive
Harry	Jack Douglas
Miss Dobbs	Patsy Rowlands
Nicholas	David Kernan
Moira	Gail Grainger
EustanceTuttle's mother	Amelia Bayntun
Fiddler	Bill Maynard

Crew list

Written by Talbot Rothwell
Music   Eric Rogers
Cinematography Alan Hume BSc
Art Director   Lionel Couch
Producer   Peter Rogers
Director   Gerald Thomas

Certificate A/PG (colour) Running time: approx. 88 minutes

Eustance Tuttle receives a torrent of last-minute instructions

CARRY ON GIRLS

'I like to think a man can have a relationship with a woman which isn't just based on sex.'
'I fully agree. She should have money as well.'

The mayor of a rundown seaside resort is all too happy to agree with Sid Fiddler's plan to stage a beauty contest in order to publicise the town and pull in the tourists. Neither man, however, has thought how this action will bring Augusta Prodworthy, a local councillor and leader of the local women's rights movement, out on the warpath. As the beauties begin to arrive, Fiddler is like a little boy in a sweetshop, much to the growing annoyance of the lady in his life, Connie Philpotts, who runs the hotel where the contestants are staying. Everything eventually comes to a head at the end of the pier where the competition is being staged, with Augusta Prodworthy leading the attack against the bikini-clad beauties.

Familiar Faces

Arnold Ridley: Private Godfrey from *Dad's Army* and also author of the play *Ghost Train*.

Robin Askwith: He went on to become the star of all the *Confessions of...* films that were made in the 1970s, the popularity of which forced the *Carry On* films to become naughtier in order to compete with *Confessions* at the box-office.

Cast list

Sidney Fiddler	Sid James
Hope Springs	Barbara Windsor
Frederick Bumble	Kenneth Connor
Connie Philpotts	Joan Sims
Peter Potter	Bernard Bresslaw
Augusta Prodworthy	June Whitfield
William	Jack Douglas
Admiral	Peter Butterworth
Mildred Bumble	Patsy Rowlands
Mrs Dukes	Joan Hickson
Paula Perkins	Valerie Leon
Larry	Robin Askwith
Dawn Brakes	Margaret Nolan
Debra	Sally Geeson
Miss Bangor	Angela Grant
Ida Downs	Wendy Richard
Police Inspector	David Lodge
Alderman Pratt	Arnold Ridley
Rosemary	Patricia Franklin
Fire chief	Bill Pertwee
Miss Drew	Marianne Stone
Constable	Billy Cornelius
Cecil Gaybody	Jimmy Logan

Crew list

Written by	Talbot Rothwell
Music	Eric Rogers
Cinematography	Alan Hume BSc
Art Director	Robert Jones
Producer	Peter Rogers
Director	Gerald Thomas

Certificate A/PG (colour)   Running time: approx. 88 minutes

Wendy Richard appears as Ida Downs (third right) with Bernard Bresslaw at the end of the line.

The Verdict

It's quite surprising that the *Carry On* team haven't come up with the idea of staging a beauty contest before, but as with *Loving* the film falls apart at the end; the pie fight being replaced by a go-kart chase. The whole tone of the gags are now obviously saucy; before this film the jokes weren't hammered home with quite such force. *Carry On Girls* was filmed on location in Brighton and it's clear the bikini-clad girls are suffering from the cold. *Girls* is by no means the worst *Carry On*; it's just average. The production rate had now fallen from three films a year to just one so obviously their popularity was now on the decline.

CARRY ON DICK

1974

'He took my most treasured possession.'
'Oh, come on, Milady, surely that went a long time ago.'

The legendary Dick Turpin, or Big Dick as he's known to his friends due to the enormous size of his weapon, is enemy Number One on Captain Fancey's list. Together with the assistance of the Bow Street Runners, led by Sergeant Jock Strapp, he is determined to bring the highwayman's reign to an end. They enlist the help of another man, the Reverend Flasher, to help them, not realising that Reverend Flasher is actually Turpin in disguise. No matter how clever Fancey thinks he is, there's just no way that he'll ever be able to get hold of Big Dick and bring him to the hangman's noose.

Familiar Faces
Sam Kelly: Comedy actor who went on to star in the sitcom *'allo, 'allo*.

The Verdict
A last hurrah? A big hit at the box-office for the film which many argue was the real end of the *Carry On*s with the subsequent departure of so many of the old retainers. *Dick* was written under extreme pressure by Rothwell and was the first one for quite some time to be based on an idea from other writers. Both James and Windsor were unhappy with the level of smut that was creeping into the scripts more and more and so decided to move on to other projects after filming this one. But does *Dick* work? After *Carry On Abroad* it was the last great *Carry On*, with the regulars all doing their best with a script that was stuffed full of *double entendres*. It was another historical romp and Rothwell was particularly inventive with

Cast list

Dick Turpin/Reverend Flasher	Sid James
Harriet/Harry	Barbara Windsor
Captain Desmond Fancey	Kenneth Williams
Martha	Hattie Jacques
Sir Roger Daley	Bernard Bresslaw
Madame Desiree	Joan Sims
Constable	Kenneth Connor
Tom	Peter Butterworth
Sergeant Jock Strapp	Jack Douglas
Mrs Giles	Patsy Rowlands
Bodkin	Bill Maynard
Lady Daley	Margaret Nolan
Isaak	John Clive
Bullock	David Lodge
Maggie	Marianne Stone
Thug	Billy Cornelius
Sir Roger Daley's coach driver	Sam Kelly
The Birds of Paradise	Linda Hooks
	Eva Reuber-Stainer
	Penny Irving
	Laraine Humphrys

Crew list

Written by Talbot Rothwell, based on a treatment by Lawrie Wyman and George Evans

Music	Eric Rogers
Cinematography	Ernest Steward BSc
Art Director	Lionel Couch
Producer	Peter Rogers
Director	Gerald Thomas

Certificate A/PG (colour) Running time: approx. 91 minutes

the historical *Carry On*s. The stars are all looking a little older but that hardly matters as they still manage to bring a degree of enthusiasm to their roles. A swansong for many, but a recommended one at that.

Highwayman Harry, alias Harriet, alias Barbara Windsor, with Dick Turpin, alias Reverend Flasher alias Sid James. Only the horses were real.

CARRY ON BEHIND

1975

'Man is injured!'
'Where? What man?'
'Is professor of archeology … Is bleeding terrible!'
'Never mind his qualifications! Is he hurt badly?'

Professor Anna Vooshka and Professor Ronald Crump are two archeologists who have the find of the decade on their hands. The trouble is it's buried under a rundown caravan holiday site owned by Major Lee. On top of all that, Professor Crump is terrified of Professor Vooshka's intentions towards him as she's made it very clear that she wants to come into his bed and do some excavating there …

Familiar Faces

Elke Sommer: German star of films such as *A Shot in the Dark* and *Zeppelin.*

Windsor Davies: Star of the classic *It Ain't Half Hot Mum* .

Ian Lavender: Yet another *Dad's Army* star joins the *Carry On* ranks.

Adrienne Post: Actress who often appeared in comedy roles, from being a child in *Hancock* to a lady with a reputation in *Till Death Us Do Part.*

Donald Hewlett: Actor whose sitcom roles include *It Ain't Half Hot Mum* and *You Rang, M'lud?*

George Layton: Writer and actor who worked throughout the 1970s on the *Doctor* series based on Richard Gordon's books.

Cast list

Professor Anna Vooshka	Elke Sommer
Professor Ronald Crump	Kenneth Williams
Arthur Upmore	Bernard Bresslaw
Major Lee	Kenneth Connor
Ernie Bragg	Jack Douglas
Daphne Barnes	Joan Sims
Mr Barnes	Peter Butterworth
Fred Ramsden	Windsor Davies
Sylvia Ramsden	Liz Fraser
Linda Upmore	Patsy Rowlands
Joe Baxter	Ian Lavender
Norma Baxter	Adrienne Post
Very Bragg	Patricia Franklin
Dean	Donald Hewlett
Sandra	Carol Hawkins
Landlord	David Lodge
Mrs Rowan	Marianne Stone
Doctor	George Layton
Bob	Brian Osborne
Clive	Larry Dann
Maureen	Diana Darvey
Veronica	Jenny Cox
Man eating salad	Billy Cornelius
Student eating ice cream	Jeremy Connor
Lady in revealing dress	Alexandra Dane
Projectionist	Sam Kelly
Plasterer	Johnny Briggs
Lady wearing hat	Lucy Griffiths

Crew list

Written by	Dave Freeman
Music	Eric Rogers
Cinematography	Ernest Steward BSc
Art Director	Lionel Couch
Producer	Peter Rogers
Director	Gerald Thomas

Certificate **AA** (later **PG**) (colour) **Running time: approx. 90 minutes**

The Verdict

A brave attempt at *Carry On Camping II.* Filmed on the same field, the only real difference is that here caravans are used instead of tents. Even though this film has had an injection of bright new talent, it's not brilliant. Repetitive in places with some very crude jokes, this was the first *Carry On* to gain a AA certificate, thereby losing a large percentage of its younger audiences and suffering as a result at the box-office. Williams, however, is on form, exposing his bottom to the camera, while Bresslaw, Butterworth and the other surviving members of the old mob go through their paces enthusiastically, trying to breathe new life into an old script. Adequate is the best way to describe this effort.

Ernie Bragg, frozen stiff in the meat freezer.

A Celebration

CARRY ON ENGLAND

'This is one of these new mixed batteries.'
'So that's what the Brigadier meant when he said that this battery was an experiment.'
'Experiment, Sir? They do not need to experiment. They gets at it right away and all the time.'

Back to the barracks! It's a battle of wits between the newly posted Captain S. Melly and the men and women of a camp where they are allowed to mix freely, in both work and play. Melly, however, has other ideas, and with the full support of Sergeant-Major Bloomer, he instigates plans to keep the sexes apart and, in his mind, heighten the effectiveness of the air defence base. Naturally enough his plans have exactly the opposite effect as members of both sexes go to extraordinary lengths to satisfy their now-forbidden urges.

Familiar Faces

Judy Geeson: Actress who starred in such films as *Fear in the Night* and *To Sir with Love*.
Patrick Mower: Action star of TV series *Target* and *Special Branch*.
Melvyn Hayes: One of the regular cast of *It Ain't Half Hot Mum* , where his character had much the same relationship with Windsor Davies as he does here.
Diane Langton: Musical star and actress who appeared in the revived *The Rag Trade*.

The Verdict

Oh dear. This neither looks nor feels like a

Cast list

Captain S. Melly	Kenneth Connor
Sergeant-Major 'Tiger' Bloomer	Windsor Davies
Sergeant Tilly Willing	Judy Geeson
Sergeant Leonard 'Len' Able	Patrick Mower
Bombardier Ready	Jack Douglas
Private Sharpe	Joan Sims
Gunner Shorthouse	Melvyn Hayes
Major Carstairs	Peter Butterworth
Private Alice Easy	Diane Langton
Major Butcher	Julian Holloway
Brigadier	Peter Jones
Captain Bull	David Lodge
Gunner Shaw	Larry Dann
Gunner Owen	Brian Osborne
Captain Melly's driver	Johnny Briggs
Corporal Cook	Patricia Franklin
Army nurse	Linda Hooks

Crew list

Written by	David Pursall and Jack Seddon
Music	Max Harris
Cinematography	Ernest Steward BSc
Art Director	Lionel Couch
Producer	Peter Rogers
Director	Gerald Thomas

Certificate AA (later **PG**) (colour) **Running time: approx. 89 minutes**

Carry On film and it did not prove to be lucrative at the box-office. The idea is pretty far-fetched and none of the new cast are really capable of the broad style of theatrics that Williams, James and Hawtrey had brought to the earlier films. Even the reliable Connor is miscast as an unlikely anti-hero instead of the usual bumbling character which he did so well. A waste of talent all round; the whole thing looks rushed and it's way, way below average.

Sergeants Tilly Willing and Len Able inspect their privates.

THAT'S CARRY ON

1977

A compilation of clips from all the *Carry On* films so far, hosted by some new linking material of Kenneth Williams and Barbara Windsor at a cinema, working the projector and sitting in the stalls watching the clips on screen.

The Verdict

Joyous celebration of the entire series, with quite a few laughs to be gained from the new linking material. It's clear that Williams and Windsor are enjoying themselves as they work together for the first time since *Carry On Dick*.

Crew list

Presented by Kenneth Williams
and Barbara Windsor
Linking sequences written by
Tony Church
Music Eric Rogers
Cinematography for linking
material Tony Imi
Producer Peter Rogers
Director Gerald Thomas

Certificate A/PG (black & white/colour)
Running time: approx. 95 minutes

CARRY ON EMMANUELLE

1978

'Why me? You can have Tom, Dick or Harry!'
'But I don't want Tom and Harry!'

Emile Prevert has a problem. After a very painful experience with a church spire while handgliding, he has not been the man he once was, and to make matters worse, his young wife, Emmanuelle Prevert, has an insatiable appetite for all things carnal - as the prime minister, the butler and an entire football team find out. In fact, wherever Emmanuelle goes, sparks fly and groins get exhausted. Nevertheless, she still longs for the love of her Emile so she devises a very clever way of getting him back into bed.

Familiar Faces

Beryl Reid: Actress of great repute, whose credits range from radio, films and TV, most recently in *Cracker*.
Henry McGee: Long-time stooge to Benny Hill.

The Verdict

This is the one that barely anybody's seen.

She'd have had plenty of leg room on a Virgin flight.

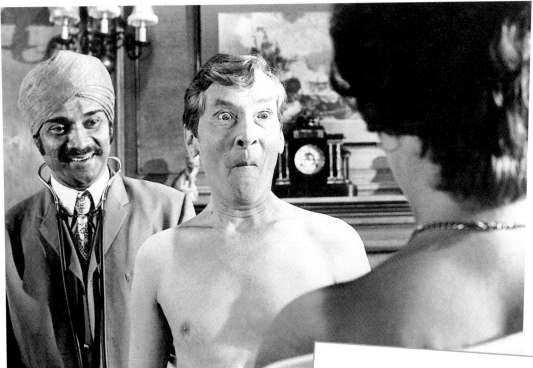

On television it's only ever been shown late at night and on video it's the one no one has heard of. This really was the death knell to the series. Part of the joy of the *Carry On* films was that they were laden with innuendo without ever showing anything naughty on screen. *Carry On Emmanuelle* sets out to redress the balance and in the process produces a comedy that's low on laughs but full of clothes dropping off and bedroom antics. Williams looks rather at a loss and even his remarkable ability with accents is strangely absent from this one. Butterworth, Sims and Douglas are given very little to do on screen while Connor plays his part straight, in marked contrast to all his other performances. See it only if curiosity gets the better of you.

Cast list

Emmanuelle Prevert	Suzanne Danielle
Emile Prevert	Kenneth Williams
Leyland	Kenneth Connor
Lyons	Jack Douglas
Mrs Dangle	Joan Sims
Richmond	Peter Butterworth
Mrs Valentine	Beryl Reid
Theodore Valentine	Larry Dann
Harold Hump	Henry McGee
Guest	Eric Barker

Crew list

Written by	Lance Peters
Music	Eric Rogers
Cinematography	Alan Hume BSc
Art Director	Jack Shampan
Producer	Peter Rogers
Director	Gerald Thomas

Certificate AA/15 (colour) Running time: approx. 90 minutes

CARRY ON COLUMBUS

'What are you looking at?'
'Sharks! Man-eating sharks!
The sea's full of them. Mind you
don't fall in!'
'My goodness! You don't think they'd eat me
whole?'
'No, I'm told they spit that out!'

I t's 1492 and the evil Sultan of Turkey controls the sea routes from the Far East to Europe. Together with his wazir he takes his pick of all the goods that pass through his land and fines anyone who dares to question his rule. A mapmaker by the name of Christopher Columbus - Chris to his friends - persuades the King and Queen of Spain to put up the money he needs to finance an expedition to chart a new route, thus avoiding the Sultan's fines. A motley collection of sailors are brought together and as the treacherous journey

Christopher Columbus protects Fatima from everything - except himself.

begins, Columbus is unaware that his new cabin boy is in fact a Turkish assassin, and a woman to boot. They eventually reach a strange new land where the natives have a vast supply of gold - or so Columbus is led to believe. His problems are, however, just beginning.

Familiar Faces

Rik Mayall: Former *Young One, New Statesman* and presents, well, *Rik Mayall Presents* for ITV. The BBC has got his *Bottom* (oo-er, Missus!).

Nigel Planer: Another *Young One* who was also seen in *Roll Over Beethoven*.

Burt Kwouk: Best remembered as Kato, Inspector Clouseau's manservant in all the *Pink Panther* films.

Tony Slattery: Comic and *Whose Line is it Anyway?* regular.

Peter Richardson: *Comic Strip Presents* actor, writer and film director.

Martin Clunes: Familiar from *Men Behaving Badly*.

Sara Crowe: The first bride from *Four Weddings and a Funeral*.

Alexei Sayle: Actor and writer whose unique humour had led him from *The Young Ones* to a show of his own and *Paris*.

Maureen Lipman: A highly acclaimed actress who will probably be best remembered for her British Telecom ads.

Holly Aird: Possibly remembered as the youngster in *The Flame Trees of Thika* but better known from *Soldier, Soldier*.

Rebecca Lacey: Daughter of supreme screen villain Ronald, she's often appeared in sitcoms on TV, most recently in *May to December*.

Richard Wilson: Victor Meldrew, of course, from *One Foot in the Grave*.

Julian Clary: Camp comedian who frequently has *Sticky Moments*.

Keith Allen: Former *Comic Strip Presents* actor who has gone on to bigger and better things, such as playing the corpse in *Shallow Grave*.

Cast list

Christopher Columbus	Jim Dale
Mordecai Mendoza	Bernard Cribbins
King Ferdinand of Spain	Leslie Phillips
Queen Isabella of Spain	June Whitfield
Fatima	Sara Crowe
Achmed	Alexei Sayle
Don Juan Felipe	Richard Wilson
Countess Esmeralda	Maureen Lipman
Don Juan Diego	Julian Clary
Pepi the Poisoner	Keith Allen
Marco the Cereal Killer	Jack Douglas
Tonto the Torch	Danny Peacock
Bart Columbus	Peter Richardson
Maria	Holly Aird
Chiquita	Rebecca Lacey
Sultan of Turkey	Rik Mayall
Wazir	Nigel Planer
Duke of Costa Brava	Jon Pertwee
Wang	Burt Kwouk
Bosun	Don Henderson
Governor of the Canaries	Peter Gilmore
Cecil the Torturer	Harold Berens
Baba the Messenger	Tony Slattery
Martin	Martin Clunes
Pontiac	Charles Fleischer
Hubba	Chris Langham
The Chief	Larry Martin
Manservant	John Antrobus

Crew list

Written by	Dave Freeman
Music	John du Prez
Cinematography	Alan Hume BSc
Production Designer	Harry Pottle
Executive Producer	Peter Rogers
Producer	John Goldstone
Director	Gerald Thomas

Certificate PG (colour) Running time: approx. 87 minutes

Don Henderson: Detective Sergeant Bullman in *The XYY Man*, *Strangers* and then *Bullman*.

Charles Fleischer: Not well known for himself but instantly recognisable as the voice of Roger Rabbit.

The Verdict

Fourteen years after *Emmanuelle*, some bright sparks thought to resurrect the series and tie it in with the anniversary of Christopher Columbus discovering America. Is it any good? Frankly, no. There are too many missing faces and for that reason alone it doesn't feel like a *Carry On*. There's a chuckle here and there and Dale is still full of that old enthusiasm, but that doesn't make up for the feeling that *Columbus* is a wasted opportunity. Nowhere as bad as *England* or *Emmanuelle* though.

For anyone who has suddenly thought, 'He's missed out *Carry On Admiral*. Surely that should be included?', the answer is no. The film in question starred David Tomlinson and Peggy Cummings and was made a year before *Carry On Sergeant* went before the cameras. It was based on a stage play called *Off the Record* and dealt with a civil servant getting a bit worse for wear in a bar with a naval lieutenant, with confusion and mayhem resulting from that encounter. High spirited and often funny, it's easily mistaken as an 'official' *Carry On* film, a notion compounded by the fact that Joan Sims starred in it as well. To date, there have been no films other than the official ones listed here that have seen production or release with the 'Carry On' prefix.

Finally, this book only deals with the *Carry On* films. All other spin-offs, TV programmes and specials are not mentioned here.

Jim Dale persuades the producer to sign his pay cheque.